CHILD HEALTH & WELL-BEING

CHILD HEALTH **&** WELL-BEING

Niamh Gaine

GILL & MACMILLAN

Gill & Macmillan
Hume Avenue
Park West
Dublin 12
with associated companies throughout the world
www.gillmacmillan.ie

© Niamh Gaine 2013

978 07171 5626 9

Print origination by Carrigboy Typesetting Services
Index by Cliff Murphy

The paper used in this book comes from the wood pulp of managed forests. For every tree felled, at least one tree is planted, thereby renewing natural resources.

A CIP catalogue record is available for this book from the British Library

For permission to reproduce photographs, the author and publisher gratefully acknowledge the following:

© Alamy: 33TL, 33TR, 47, 49, 53, 54, 58, 62, 64, 75, 83; © Department of Education and Skills: 11; © Department of Health and Children: 115, 118; © Food Dudes: 24; © Getty Images: 33B, 50, 51; ©NCCA: 14; © safefoods: 100, 150.

The author and publisher have made every effort to trace all copyright holders, but if any has been inadvertently overlooked we would be pleased to make the necessary arrangement at the first opportunity.

This book is dedicated with love and affection
to the memory of Betty Foley
(1921–2011)

Acknowledgements

So many people had an impact on the writing of this book, it would be impossible to mention all of them.

Thanks to my family, who put up with me during the writing and editing of the book. Thanks to my Mum, Liz, my Dad, John, and Carol, Seán and Bill for the tea, support and proof-reading assistance. Many thanks to all those who guided and encouraged me during all my years of study.

Thanks to all my friends at home and abroad for the support and encouragement, tea sessions, chats and laughs! You know who you are.

Thanks to the many students whose contributions over the years have helped to shape this book.

This book could never have been written without the support and encouragement of Cork College of Commerce and in particular the amazing women in the childcare department. This book owes a huge debt of gratitude to staff members past and present who have mentored and helped me over the last few years. I truly am standing on the shoulders of giants!

Special thanks to Marion and the team at Gill & Macmillan for giving me the opportunity to fulfil the long-cherished dream of writing a book.

Contents

Section One: Legislation, Health and Welfare

Chapter One: Legislation and Policy 3
Chapter Two: Health in the ECCE Setting. 16
Chapter Three: Common Childhood Illnesses 41
Chapter Four: Personal Care Routines in ECCE 69

Section Two: Nutrition, Health and Safety

Chapter Five: Nutrition in the ECCE Setting 91
Chapter Six: Safety in the ECCE Setting. 120

Section Three: Health Promotion

Chapter Seven: Promoting a Healthy Environment in an ECCE Setting. . . . 147
Chapter Eight: Applying Developmental Knowledge to Promote
    Child Health and Well-being. 162

Section Four: Appendices

Appendix I: Sample Letter Informing Parents of the Outbreak of an
    Infectious Disease in the Setting 173
Appendix II: Exclusion Periods for ECCE Settings 175
Appendix III: Child Health and Well-being Module: Assessment 176

Bibliography 183
Index 187

Section One

LEGISLATION, HEALTH AND WELFARE

chapter one

Legislation and Policy

LEARNING OUTCOMES

After reading this chapter you will be:

▶ familiar with the legislation governing children's health and well-being in Ireland

▶ aware of the implications for child health and well-being of Síolta and Aistear.

INTRODUCTION

Before we can begin to explore the factors affecting child health and well-being we must first examine the legislation governing children's welfare in Ireland. This chapter gives a brief overview of the following:

▶ UN Convention on the Rights of the Child (1989)
▶ Childcare Act 1991
▶ Child Care (Pre-School Services) (No. 2) Regulations 2006
▶ Safety, Health and Welfare at Work Act 2005
▶ *Children First* (1999) and *Our Duty to Care* (2002)
▶ Disability Act 2005.

Please note that an in-depth discussion of each piece of legislation is beyond the remit of this book. Interested readers are directed to *The Best Interests of the Child* (McPartland 2010) for a comprehensive overview of how Irish law impacts on the lives of children, their parents/guardians and early child care and education (ECCE) workers.

UN CONVENTION ON THE RIGHTS OF THE CHILD (1989)

The UN Convention on the Rights of the Child, which was drawn up in 1989, outlines the basic rights of children worldwide. As McPartland (2010) points out, the Convention is not itself a piece of legislation, but it has influenced Irish legislation since its ratification. The Convention is governed by four basic principles:

1   **Non-discrimination.** All children, without exception, are entitled to all the rights in the Convention.

2   **Devotion to the best interests of the child.** Those working with children have a responsibility to put children's interests first.

3   **The right to life, survival and development.** All children have the right to live and to healthy development.

4   **Respect for the views of the child.** Children must be treated with respect and their views and opinions listened to and taken into account. This means that we must try to include children in in our decision-making processes and allow them to make choices. For example, children should be given some opportunities for free play and to choose their own activities during the day.

CHILDCARE ACT 1991

The Childcare Act 1991 was the first piece of Irish legislation to focus on children. It defines a child as someone who is under 18 years of age (unless they are married). The Act is an extensive piece of legislation, and it is not within the remit of this text to discuss all aspects of it. For our purposes we will focus on Part VII of the Act, which defines a pre-school child and pre-school service.

Pre-school child: a child under six years of age who is not attending a national school or school providing an educational programme similar to a national school.

Pre-school service: any pre-school, playgroup, day nursery, crèche, daycare or other similar service which caters for pre-school children. These include sessional, full time and drop-in services.

Under the Childcare Act, pre-school providers must notify the Health Service Executive (HSE) that they are operating a pre-school and HSE inspection teams are obliged to supervise and inspect pre-schools. The Child Care (Pre-School Services) (No. 2) Regulations 2006 outline the requirements for a pre-school setting and are currently the most important piece of legislation governing ECCE settings.

CHILD CARE (PRE-SCHOOL SERVICES) (No. 2) REGULATIONS 2006

The Pre-School Regulations are both a tool for settings to ensure that they meet legislative requirements and a checking instrument for the HSE inspection teams to assess services. Each ECCE setting is inspected once a year to ensure that it complies with the Childcare Act and Regulations, and HSE reports are made available to the public. The regulations govern all pre-school services, as defined by the Childcare Act. There are 32 regulations in all, most of which are concerned with providing a safe environment for children attending ECCE services. The regulations fall into five areas (Donohoe & Gaynor 2011).

1 Health, welfare and development of the child.
2 Notification and inspection by the HSE.
3 Record keeping.
4 Standard of premises and facilities.
5 General administration.

It is not the purpose of this section to give a detailed account of all 32 regulations. Some of the key regulations for children's health and well-being are summarised below. For further information on the regulations, readers are directed to McPartland (2010) or Donohoe and Gaynor (2011).

Administration of medication and first aid

ECCE settings are required to have a suitable first aid box in each room of the pre-school and a first aid box must be taken on outings. There must be at least one trained first aider available at all times and on all outings. Any medication must be clearly labelled and inaccessible to children. Written parental consent is needed to administer medication to children or to arrange medical assistance for children.

Staffing requirements

The regulations set down the adult:child ratio considered suitable for each type of service in order to give children individual attention and to keep them safe. Settings *must* adhere to these ratios. Work experience students are not counted for the purpose of the adult:child ratio.

Table 1.1 Adult:child ratios: full- and part-time daycare

Age range	Adult:child ratio	Maximum group size
0–1	1:3	9
1–2	1:5	10
2–3	1:6	12
3–6	1:8	24

Table 1.2 Adult:child ratios: sessional services

Age	Adult:child ratio	Maximum group size
0–1	1:3	9
1–2.5	1:5	10
2.6–6	1:10*	20*

*For the pre-school room the ratio for services providing a free pre-school year session has been increased to 1:11. The 1:11 ratio was introduced by the government in the 2011 budget, raising the ratio from the previous 1:10 and the maximum group size from 20 to 22. This increase *only* applies to the free pre-school year session: for the rest of the day and for services not providing the free pre-school year the standard ratios apply.

THINK ABOUT IT

Do you think the adult:child ratios are adequate for the age of the children involved? Why/why not?

Record keeping

The regulations describe the documentation and records that must be kept by pre-school services. When the inspectorate team visits a setting they will ask to see these records and expect them to be completed accurately. The following records are required by the regulations:

▶ a register listing details of each child attending the setting
▶ a register containing staff details, including name, position, qualifications and experience

- information about the type of service being provided and the age range of children attending the service
- facilities provided
- opening hours
- fees
- policies and procedures
- daily attendance records
- daily staff rosters
- details of medicine administered to children
- details of any accidents and injuries
- arrival and departure times of children
- arrival and departure times of staff
- records of programmes offered to children.

Accurate and up-to-date records are essential in an ECCE setting. Records help to ensure that the setting is complying with health and safety requirements. Parents are entitled to view any records kept on their child. It is recommended that records concerning the care of individual children are kept until the child is 21 in case any queries should arise after the child leaves the setting.

SAFETY, HEALTH AND WELFARE AT WORK ACT 2005

This is a general piece of legislation relating to workplaces in general. The Act does not specifically relate to ECCE settings, but all ECCE settings must comply with the requirements of the Act. The Act sets out the responsibilities of both employees and employers in creating and maintaining a safe work environment.

The responsibilities of the **employer** (ECCE manager) are to:

- manage work activities to ensure the safety, health and welfare of employees at work
- design, improve and maintain a safe place of work
- use equipment that is safe
- reduce risk and prevent accidents by implementing, providing and maintaining safe systems of work
- provide information, training and supervision to ensure that safety standards are met
- provide appropriate protective clothing and equipment

- produce and implement a safety statement that outlines safety procedures and emergency plans
- appoint a competent person as the organisation's safety officer.

The responsibilities of the **employee** (ECCE worker) are to:

- follow safety guidelines and wear protective equipment
- take reasonable care in performing their duties so that they do not affect the health and safety of others
- report any unsafe conditions to a supervisor
- undergo any reasonable medical or other assessment if required by their employer (Donohoe & Gaynor 2011).

Under the Safety, Health and Welfare at Work Act 2005 every place of work must draw up a **safety statement** outlining how the organisation will maintain a safe workplace, identifying any hazards and risks in the workplace and outlining how these risks should be dealt with. The safety statement should:

- identify workplace hazards and levels of safety required
- assess the risks arising from such hazards
- identify the steps to be taken to deal with these risks
- identify the resources necessary to implement and maintain safety standards
- indicate necessary precautions to prevent accidents
- document the names and responsibilities of safety representatives
- specify the reporting procedure to be used in the event of an accident.

If an ECCE centre complies with the Safety, Health and Welfare at Work Act and takes a proactive approach to preventing workplace accidents, it should be safe for workers, children and their parents/guardians.

CHILDREN FIRST AND OUR DUTY TO CARE

Children First: National Guidelines for the Protection and Welfare of Children (1999, updated 2011, hereafter referred to as *Children First*) was published by the government in response to various child abuse scandals.

Our Duty to Care (2002) was published for the voluntary sector and outlines the same procedures as *Children First*. *Children First* outlines the procedure to be followed in cases of suspected abuse.

Recognising and reporting child abuse

If child abuse is suspected, *Children First* recommends a three-step procedure.

1   Consider the possibility that abuse has occurred.
2   Observe the signs that indicate abuse has occurred.
3   Record all information in as much detail as you can.

Any person who has suspicions that abuse is occurring has a duty to report their suspicions. Suspicions might be aroused by the following.

- A specific indication from the child.
- A statement of a witness or the presence of illness/injury/behaviour consistent with abuse.
- A symptom not totally consistent with abuse which is supported by other evidence of harm and neglect.
- Consistent signs of neglect over a period of time.

Suspicions of abuse must be accompanied by **objective signs** of abuse. *Children First* explains in detail what types of behaviour and signs are considered to be objective signs of abuse. If abuse is suspected, a report must be made to the duty social worker at the HSE in person, in writing or over the phone. It is helpful if the person who first becomes suspicious or who witnessed the abuse makes the report. If it is an emergency and the duty social worker cannot be contacted, the Gardaí must be informed.

The report should contain:

- the name and address of the child/parents and other children in the family
- the name and address of the alleged abuser
- a full account of the concern about the child's safety
- the date(s) of incidents
- the circumstances of incidents
- any explanation offered for any injuries
- the child's own statement
- any protective factors in place
- the name of the child's school and GP
- the reporter's own connection to the child
- any action that has already been taken

◗ any other agencies involved

◗ the name of the person who is reporting the concern.

Children First was published as a set of guidelines for those working with children: its recommendations are not statutory obligations. At the time of writing a bill is being drafted to place *Children First* on a statutory footing: the consultation process is currently under way. If the bill is passed it will mean that if those working with children have suspicions about a child's welfare or if a disclosure is made, the worker will have a legal obligation to report the suspicions/disclosure.

DISABILITY ACT 2005

Since the late 1990s much legislation has been passed relating to people with special educational needs. The 2005 Disability Act defines a disability as:

> **A substantial restriction in the capacity of the person which is permanent or likely to be permanent, to carry out a profession, business or occupation in the State or to participate in the social or cultural life of the State by reason of an enduring physical, sensory, mental health or intellectual impairment. (p. 6)**

Under the Disability Act parents can request that an assessment of the child's needs be carried out. From this an assessment of needs report will be drawn up, which will include the following information:

◗ whether the person has a disability

◗ the nature and extent of the disability

◗ the health and education needs arising from that disability

◗ the services considered appropriate to those needs and the timescale ideally required for their delivery

◗ when a review of assessment should take place.

The Act also provides that people with disabilities should have access to public buildings, services and information (though places where this would not be practicable or the costs would be too high are excluded from this requirement).

POLICY DEVELOPMENTS IN ECCE

Two important policy developments in the ECCE sector are *Síolta: the National Quality Framework for Early Childhood Education*, published in 2006 by the Centre for Early Childhood Development and Education (CEDCE), and *Aistear: the Early Childhood Curriculum Framework*, published in 2009 by the National Council for Curriculum and Assessment (NCCA). This section will enable you to understand how Síolta and Aistear promote children's health and well-being in an ECCE setting.

Síolta

Síolta: the National Quality Framework for Early Childhood Education (CECDE 2006) outlines the principles and underlying standards required for a quality ECCE setting. Síolta is designed to be used in all services for children aged 0–6 years, including childminding services, pre-school services and the junior classes in primary school. Síolta outlines 16 **standards**, which are aims that services must meet. Each standard is broken down into **components**, which provide guidance to enable settings to meet the standards. Three standards are particularly relevant for child health and well-being:

síolta
The National Quality Framework for Early Childhood Education

▶ Standard Two: Environment
▶ Standard Nine: Health and Welfare
▶ Standard Fifteen: Legislation and Regulation.

Standard Two: Environment

This standard states that:

> **Enriching environments both indoor and outdoor (including materials and equipment) [should be] well maintained, safe, available, accessible, adaptable, developmentally appropriate and offer a variety of challenging and stimulating experiences. (CEDCE 2006:19)**

This requires ECCE workers to provide a challenging but safe environment that allows children to take risks and explore their developing abilities. The importance of a well-designed and attractive environment is highlighted. Regular safety checks will need to be carried out to ensure compliance with legislation and to make sure that the environment remains safe for children. The environment must be accessible to children of all abilities, including children with special educational needs. Regular inspection, cleaning checks and reflective practice combine to ensure that settings meet the standard of 'Environment'.

THINK ABOUT IT

How can adults provide a safe but challenging environment for young children?

Standard Nine: Health and Welfare

The Health and Welfare standard states that:

Promoting the health and welfare of the child requires protection from harm, provision of nutritious food, appropriate opportunities for rest and secure relationships characterized by trust and respect. (CEDCE 2006:65)

Standard Nine involves four aspects:

1 protecting children from harm
2 nutrition
3 providing opportunities for children to rest and sleep
4 emphasising the role of secure relationships in the ECCE setting.

The setting should devise and implement a wide range of policies and procedures to promote health and safety. Appendix One of *Síolta* lists 36 policies that should be followed by ECCE settings to meet this standard. Chapter Six of this book will explore the policies and procedures in an ECCE setting in more detail. Both the FETAC Child Health and Well-being module and this textbook cover each aspect of Standard Nine in detail: see Chapters Five (nutrition), Six (safety), Seven (providing opportunities for rest and sleep in the ECCE setting) and Eight (attachment and secure relationships between adults and children).

Standard Fifteen: Legislation and Regulation

Meeting the standard of Legislation and Regulation 'requires that all relevant regulations and legislative requirements are met or exceeded' (CEDCE 2006:101).

Settings are required to keep up to date with changes in legislation and to have procedures in place to facilitate this. ECCE settings are governed by a wide range of legislation, not only the legislation covered earlier in this chapter, but also legislation relating to employment, equality, and health and safety.

CASE STUDY: SÍOLTA IN ACTION

(*Note:* the numbers in brackets refer to the relevant standard and component of Síolta. For example, 2.1 refers to Standard 2, Component 1.)

Sunshine Pre-school is a full-time daycare centre catering for 20 children aged 2–5 years, in three rooms. It is a purpose-built facility designed to meet the needs of the children who attend and the adults who work in the centre (2.1). The setting is fully compliant with all legislation (15.1) including buildings legislation, meaning that the setting is fully accessible for wheelchair users (2.2). The centre is run by Mary and a team of four staff. Mary and her staff operate a key worker system allowing children to form bonds of attachment with individual carers (9.6). There is a purpose-built sleep room (9.5) and an outdoor area where the children spend a minimum of half an hour every day, depending on the weather (2.1). The outdoor area is well stocked with a wide range of equipment including a covered sand pit, large apparatus including swings, slide and see-saw and ride-on tractors and cars (2.5). The outdoor area is fenced off, with a childproof gate securing the area (2.4). As required by legislation and Síolta, the setting has devised a wide range of policies and procedures (9.1, 9.2). All staff are Garda vetted and have completed Children First training (9.2). Regular fire drills are held (9.7) in order to prepare children for emergency situations. The setting operates a healthy eating policy and runs a Healthy Eating week each year to promote healthy eating in the setting (9.4). Sunshine Pre-school uses the standards of Síolta to ensure that children's *health and welfare* is promoted in a safe and appropriate *environment* and in line with all relevant *legislation*.

Aistear

Aistear is the curriculum framework for all children from birth to six years. Like Síolta, Aistear is designed to be used in a range of settings including childminding settings, sessional services, full- and part-time daycare settings, infant classes in primary schools and children's own homes. Aistear aims to help children to

Creatchuraclam na Luath-Óige
The Early Childhood Curriculum Framework

grow and develop as confident and competent learners and is based around four themes, each with four aims and 24 learning goals. The four **themes** of Aistear are: Well-being; Identity and Belonging; Communication and Exploring; and Thinking. The theme of Well-being is most relevant to the area of children's health and well-being.

The four aims of the theme of Well-being are that children will:

1   be strong psychologically and socially
2   be as healthy and fit as they can be
3   be creative and spiritual
4   develop a positive outlook on learning and on life.

The theme of Well-being takes a broad view of the definition of well-being. It includes not only physical and psychological well-being but also creative, spiritual and social well-being and intellectual curiosity. The theme of Well-being involves wellness in the full sense of the word.

Psychological and *social* well-being are linked together. In an ECCE setting, this involves developing attachment relationships, helping children to deal with their emotions and feelings and to handle transitions in their lives, including being apart from their parents, moving between rooms in the setting and moving from the setting to school.

Physical well-being is covered in Aim Two: children should be as healthy and fit as they can be (NCCA 2009:17). Physical well-being includes the development of gross and fine motor skills and self-care skills. ECCE settings must help children to become self-sufficient and master such skills as self-feeding, putting on and taking off their own coat, and toilet training, so that they are ready for the transition to Junior Infants.

Creativity and *spirituality* means encouraging children to explore the arts and the environment around them. Spirituality does not mean that the ECCE worker must teach the customs and beliefs of a particular religion; rather it involves teaching children a sense of 'wonder and awe' about the world around them and a respect for all beliefs.

The final aspect of well-being – *intellectual curiosity* – involves encouraging children to have a sense of curiosity about the world and an interest in learning. Children should be encouraged to engage in active learning and to develop confidence in their own abilities.

CASE STUDY: WELL-BEING IN ACTION

(*Note:* the numbers in brackets relate to the relevant sections in Aistear's Well-being theme.)

Sunshine Pre-school meets Aistear's theme of Well-being. The routine is designed to ensure that children have enough time for rest, nutrition and play (2.6). A key worker system is in operation, helping children to feel secure in the setting (1.1). The setting has a policy on helping children to handle transitions: when a new child begins in the pre-school their parents can spend time in the setting to help the child feel at ease. Workers will also help children through transitions in their lives by talking and listening to them. An end of year celebration is held to celebrate children's transition from the setting to primary school (1.3).

Sunshine Pre-school offers a play-based curriculum (3.2). The weekly plan includes time for art and craft (3.1) and physical activities including music and movement (2.1, 2.2). Circle time is held daily to allow children space to discuss their feelings (1.2) and to introduce topics such as self-care skills (2.4), healthy eating (2.6) and keeping children safe (2.5). A mix of child- and adult-directed activities are planned, allowing children time to make choices (4.1, 4.6); and in doing so the setting enables children to learn to make decisions for themselves and be confident in their own abilities (1.6, 3.4, 4.6). By planning around the theme of Well-being, Sunshine Pre-school is preparing children to enter primary school as 'confident, happy and healthy' individuals.

Signpost for reflection

What elements of the Pre-School Regulations, Síolta and Aistear have you observed in action in your work placement? Do you think the legislation that is in place creates the best environment for young children?

chapter two

Health in the ECCE Setting

After reading this chapter you will:

- be able to define 'health'
- be aware of the determinants and dimensions of health
- be familiar with the concepts of health education and health promotion
- understand the factors that can affect children's health
- be familiar with the vaccination schedule for children in Ireland.

INTRODUCTION

In this chapter you will develop a broad understanding of the concept of health. You will become familiar with the factors affecting health and the common signs and symptoms of illness: as an ECCE worker, you must be able to identify the signs and symptoms of common childhood illnesses. This chapter will provide you with the knowledge and skills to promote children's health.

WHAT IS HEALTH?

It can be difficult to define exactly what we mean by health. Health is a broad concept that can include any of the following:

- eating healthily
- exercising regularly
- absence of illness
- engaging in health-promoting behaviours, for example not smoking.

THINK ABOUT IT

What do you think of when you think of health and being healthy?

The most commonly cited definition of health is that of the World Health Organisation (WHO): 'A state of complete physical, mental and social well-being, not merely the absence of disease or infirmity' (WHO 1946).

According to this definition, health involves more than the absence of disease or illness. It involves *wellness*, a state of positive physical and mental health. This fuller definition of health is the view taken in the FETAC Child Health and Well-being module and in this book. Chapters Seven and Eight in particular examine how to promote physical and emotional well-being in an ECCE setting.

DETERMINANTS OF HEALTH

Health is determined by three factors:

1 social and economic environment
2 physical environment
3 a person's individual characteristics.

Each determinant has an effect on an individual's health. A person's own characteristics and health behaviours such as diet, exercise, smoking or non-smoking have an immediate effect on their health. The physical environment also has an effect: for example, a rural environment may be healthier than an urban environment in which there are high levels of car exhaust fumes, etc. The social and economic environment of an area also has an impact on a person's health. Countries or areas with good social services and supports promote better health for those living in the area.

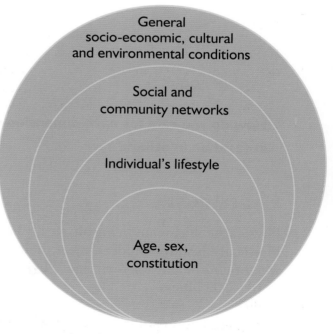

Figure 2.1 Determinants of health

DIMENSIONS OF HEALTH

Health consists of six different aspects or **dimensions**. All six aspects combine to create a sense of wellness and health.

Figure 2.2 Dimensions of health

THINK ABOUT IT

How do you rate for each dimension of health? Are you healthier in some areas than in others?

Physical health

Physical health means being physically healthy, with normal growth and development. Physically healthy children meet their developmental milestones and are a normal weight and height for their age. Physical health also implies the absence of disease or physical illness.

Emotional health

Emotional health involves being able to identify, acknowledge and express our emotions appropriately and being able to identify, acknowledge and respond to others' emotions. The *National Children's Strategy* describes children's emotional health as involving their 'feelings and actions … [a] growing ability to adapt to change, to cope with stress and to demonstrate self-control. It also involves children's ability to empathise with others and behave in a socially responsible manner' (DoHC 2000:35). Emotionally healthy children are able to recognise their own emotions and express them in an age-appropriate manner.

Mental health

Mental health involves being able to organise our thoughts logically and implies the absence of mental illness. Mental health is strongly linked to emotional health and social health. The WHO defines mental health as 'a state of well-being in which every individual realises his or her own potential, can cope with the normal stresses of life, can work productively and fruitfully and is able to make a contribution to the community' (WHO 2011). We can promote children's mental health and well-being by helping them to develop coping skills in early childhood and encouraging each child to fulfil their potential.

Social health

This refers to the way we relate to other people and form relationships. The *National Children's Strategy* sees social relationships as important: 'From an early age, but with increasing significance as they grow older, children require formal and informal opportunities to play and socialise with their peers of both sexes' (DoHC 2000:35). As children grow, developing and maintaining friendships becomes important. The ECCE worker should encourage the development of social relationships by providing opportunities for co-operative play.

Spiritual health

Spiritual health involves the development of personal and moral codes of conduct. For some children it also involves religious beliefs and practices, although some parents may decide against raising their child in a formal religion. Spiritual development is recognised as important by the *National Children's Strategy* (DoHC 2000). Spiritual health involves developing a sense of awe and wonder in the world, the development of a moral code and being able to tell right from wrong. ECCE workers can help children to develop spiritual health by teaching them moral codes, for example 'don't lie' and 'respect others'. This can be done in story time; many traditional stories teach young children moral codes. For example, Goldilocks and the Three Bears teaches children to respect others' property.

Environmental health

This refers to the general health of the particular area in which we live. For example, the environmental health of a rural society would probably be very different from the environmental health of an urban, industrial society. A child in a rural community will be exposed to fresh air, few pollutants and will have space for outdoor play. A child in an urban environment will be exposed to more environmental pollutants and may not have access to space for outdoor play. Environmental health also varies from country to country. For example, since the nuclear reactor disaster in 1986 Chernobyl in Ukraine has experienced poor environmental health.

HEALTH EDUCATION AND HEALTH PROMOTION

As an ECCE worker it is your responsibility to educate children about their health and to promote healthy behaviours and practices. You are a health educator and health promoter and will be involved in teaching children many basic health behaviours, such as hand washing and eating healthily. There are three types of health education: primary, secondary and tertiary.

- **Primary health education** involves giving information and advice on staying healthy. ECCE workers are involved in primary health education when they teach children about hand washing, healthy eating, exercise and other health behaviours. An example of primary health education is organising a healthy eating week in the ECCE setting.
- **Secondary health education** relates to the early detection and treatment of conditions in order to prevent further complications or the illness becoming worse. ECCE workers are involved in secondary health education when they notice children developing the signs and symptoms of illness.
- **Tertiary health education** involves limiting the impact of chronic conditions by teaching the child about the condition, its impact and management. As an ECCE worker you may be involved in the care of a child with a chronic illness such as asthma. You can talk to the child about the illness and help to educate them about the condition.

Health education can be undertaken in a variety of ways. Some approaches are more suited to the role of the ECCE worker than others.

CASE STUDY: HEALTH EDUCATION IN ECCE

Jane is an ECCE worker at Little Rascals pre-school. In her role in the setting, Jane is involved in primary, secondary and tertiary health education. When Jane and her colleagues set out the curriculum for the term they plan some opportunities for *primary health education*. This involves events such as Healthy Eating Week and teaching children about hand washing and exercise. Daily circle time is often used as a tool for talking about these topics and for discussing children's feelings.

Jane is also involved in *secondary health education*; in the course of her daily work she notices children who begin to show signs and symptoms of illness. Jane was involved in dealing with a recent outbreak of chickenpox in the setting. When Tom came into pre-school he seemed 'off form', tired and irritable. Later in the day Jane noticed a rash on Tom's arms. She immediately isolated Tom from the other children and brought him to the quiet room where he could rest. She notified Tom's parents, who took Tom to the doctor, who confirmed that Tom had chickenpox. Jane then sent a letter to the parents of the other children in the setting notifying them that there had been a case of chickenpox in the setting.

Jane has recently been involved in *tertiary health* education in her role of key worker for Gina. Gina is four years old and has recently been diagnosed with asthma. In co-operation with Gina's parents, Jane has talked about asthma, in a way that Gina and the other children can understand, during circle time. She also administers Gina's inhalers when necessary and talks to Gina about the importance of listening to her body and using her inhaler when she needs it.

APPROACHES TO HEALTH EDUCATION

Figure 2.3 The various approaches to health education

There are a number of different approaches to health education.

- **Medical:** This involves preventing illness through public health measures, e.g. screening and vaccination. ECCE workers should be aware of these measures, but they are not involved in their delivery: this is the responsibility of the public health team.

- **Educational:** This involves providing the information and skills to enable children's parents to make informed choices about their children's health. ECCE workers may be involved in this by providing literature and brochures at the setting. The Health Promotion Unit provides useful leaflets about child safety, immunisations, sudden infant death syndrome (SIDS) prevention, childhood illnesses, etc.

- **Behavioural change:** Based on the behavioural theory of B. F. Skinner, a psychologist who believed that humans learn through reward and punishment, this approach helps people develop new skills by rewarding good behaviour. For example, a setting might use a star chart to reward children who are regularly eating fruit and vegetables. The Food Dudes programme, which is described in more detail later in the chapter, is an example of a behavioural change programme.

- **Fear creation:** This involves using 'scare tactics' and is common in the media, for example headlines such as 'Obesity a ticking time bomb'. These headlines are useful in grabbing people's attention but can sometimes lead to scaremongering and panic. The fear creation approach is useful for getting a strong message across. For example, the media's coverage of the swine flu crisis encouraged people to observe good hygiene practices, which helped to prevent the virus escalating. However, this approach should be used sparingly, so that it does not lose its effectiveness.

▶ **Empowerment:** This approach aims to help people develop the skills, confidence and self-esteem to make changes in their lives and become healthier. For example, the empowerment approach would educate children about exercise and provide opportunities for exercise.

HEALTH PROMOTION

Health promotion has been defined as 'The process of enabling people to increase their control over and improve their health' (WHO 1986).

Health promotion can be undertaken on a formal basis, targeting a specific group at a certain time, for example an ECCE worker deciding to promote hand washing as part of the curriculum plan for the week. It can also be done informally, on a one to one basis or through television or the media in general. Children learn by example and the ECCE worker needs to be a positive role model for children; there is little point in teaching children about hand washing or healthy eating if we are not seen to do the same. Therefore the ECCE worker must take care to follow the same rules we expect children to adhere to.

Health promoters include:

▶ the WHO
▶ the HSE
▶ teachers and educators
▶ the media
▶ national voluntary organisations and pressure groups
▶ dentists
▶ GPs and district nurses
▶ Gardaí
▶ the fire brigade.

Topics for health education and health promotion in an ECCE setting include:

▶ healthy eating
▶ our bodies

▶ exercise
▶ care of teeth
▶ sun awareness
▶ hand washing.

EXERCISE

How would you plan a week's healthy eating theme in an ECCE setting? Make a list of activities you could run and research books and materials you could use to support the topic.

Food Dudes

Food Dudes is a popular health promotion initiative funded by Bord Bia and run in many Irish primary schools. The Food Dudes programme, devised by Bangor University in Wales, uses a rewards system, based on the principles of behavioural psychology, to encourage children to eat more fruit and vegetables. The programme is divided into two phases.

Phase 1 is an intensive 16-day programme which introduces children to the Food Dudes, four superheroes who gain special powers from eating fruit and vegetables. The Food Dudes battle the Junk Punks, baddies who want to drain the world of energy by depriving people of fruit and vegetables. During Phase 1 the children watch DVDs telling the story of the Food Dudes and get letters from the Food Dudes. Each day children in the class are asked to try a new fruit or vegetable. As a reward for trying the food the children are given prizes of Food Dude merchandise, such as rulers, erasers and lunchboxes.

Phase 2 extends the Food Dudes programme to the home. Children are encouraged to bring in fruit and vegetables from home for their lunch. A wall chart is used to log the children's progress and targets are set, with more prizes available for reaching certain targets.

Does Food Dudes work?

Yes! Bord Bia, in association with University College Dublin, has conducted an extended pilot study of the effectiveness of Food Dudes in 150 primary schools. The Food Dudes programme was found to increase the amount of fruit and vegetables brought to school by children and increased the amount of fruit and vegetables actually eaten in school. Food Dudes works on two levels: it encourages children to adopt the habit of eating fruit and vegetables; and it teaches them about the benefits of eating fruit and vegetables.

FACTORS AFFECTING CHILDREN'S HEALTH

Children's health is influenced by many factors, which combine to affect children's health throughout the lifespan. This section looks at each factor in turn and discusses its influence on child health.

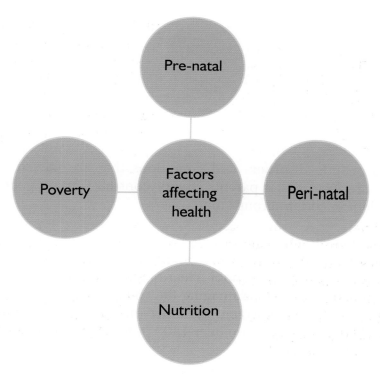

Figure 2.4 Factors influencing children's health

Pre-natal factors

Several factors affecting children's health are pre-natal: events or incidents that occur during pregnancy, **before** the child is born. Figure 2.5 illustrates some of the most important pre-natal factors that can affect a child's health.

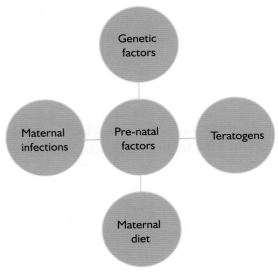

Figure 2.5 Pre-natal factors

Genetic factors

Genetic factors include disorders and conditions that are passed down through families. These are factors that parents cannot control. Certain genetic conditions are more prevalent in certain groups than others.

Cystic fibrosis is most common among Western Europeans and in particular in Ireland, which has the highest rate in the world. A child with cystic fibrosis produces sticky mucus that their body cannot clear, making them more susceptible to infections. The mucus builds up, damaging the child's internal organs, in particular the lungs. The average life expectancy for a person with cystic fibrosis in Ireland is late twenties/early thirties. There are over 1,100 people with cystic fibrosis in Ireland (Flood 2010a).

Sickle cell disorder is an inherited blood condition. Sickle cell disorder causes the body's red blood cells to change from a round to a crescent shape during what is called a **crisis**. This is extremely painful and will leave the child incapacitated until the crisis has passed. The red blood cells will be short-lived, which results in anaemia. Sickle cell anaemia occurs among people of African origin. Currently about 400 children in Ireland have sickle cell anaemia (Flood 2010a).

CASE STUDY: CYSTIC FIBROSIS

John is three years old and attends Little Treasures nursery on a part-time basis. When John was born the heel prick test was performed, the results of which indicated that there was a high risk that John had cystic fibrosis. This was followed by the sweat test, which involves taking a sample of sweat from the leg or armpit and testing for salt levels. The sweat test revealed that John has cystic fibrosis. John's parents were shocked by the results; neither had realised that they were carriers of the cystic fibrosis gene. John attends the nearby hospital, where he is cared for by a team of specialists. The dietician has prescribed a high-calorie diet and enzyme supplements for John to take with every meal to aid his digestion. The physiotherapist taught John's parents how to do chest clapping exercises in order to clear his chest of mucus.

John's parents were nervous about sending John to pre-school but decided it would be good for him to mix with other children. They visited the local service and after discussion with staff there were more than happy to enrol him for three mornings a week. Lisa was assigned as John's key worker. She had studied cystic fibrosis in college and now began refreshing her knowledge with extra research. She learned how to administer John's physiotherapy so that she could perform the exercises in setting. Cross-infection is a very dangerous risk for children with cystic fibrosis, so Lisa and her co-workers have revised the cleaning schedule and are extra vigilant with hygiene methods. Three months in and John is very happy at Little Treasures.

Some genetic conditions are carried on the X chromosome. Girls have two X chromosomes, so girls who have the affected chromosome will not develop the condition. However, they may be carriers of the condition and are at risk of passing it to their children. Boys have one X chromosome and one Y chromosome, so boys who are born with the affected X chromosome will develop the condition. Examples of conditions carried on the X chromosome include:

- **Muscular dystrophy** – a condition in which the body's muscles weaken instead of getting stronger. Muscular dystrophy affects 1 in 3,500 male births in Ireland (Flood 2010a).
- **Haemophilia** – a condition in which the child's blood does not clot properly, resulting in profuse bleeding. Haemophilia affects 1 in 5,000 baby boys in Ireland (Flood 2010a).

Teratogens

A teratogen is anything that can potentially cause a birth defect or negatively affect the development of the unborn child. The damage caused by the teratogen depends on the stage at which the unborn baby is exposed to it. Teratogens cause the most damage during the first three months of pregnancy. There are many different teratogens; the table below illustrates the effects of some of the most serious.

Table 2.1 Common teratogens and their effects on the child

Teratogen	Possible effects
Smoking tobacco	Low birth weight
	Premature birth
	Sudden infant death syndrome (SIDS)
Drinking alcohol	Heavy drinking during pregnancy can cause foetal alcohol syndrome (FAS)
	Moderate drinking has been associated with attention problems
Illegal drug use (e.g. marijuana, cocaine, heroin)	Associated with birth defects, attention problems and developmental delay in babies
	Babies may be born with an addiction to the drug
Legal drug use	Some legal drugs such as aspirin are harmful to the unborn child and should not be used during pregnancy

Maternal diet

During pregnancy mothers should avoid certain foods and increase their intake of others to promote optimal foetal growth and development. For example, expectant mothers are advised to avoid foods such as uncooked shellfish and unpasteurised milk because of the risk of contracting salmonella.

It is recommended that expectant mothers increase their intake of folic acid (a B vitamin found in green leafy vegetables and cereals) for three months before and three months after conception. Taking folic acid during pregnancy has been found to be a protective factor for spina bifida and other neural tube defects. Spina bifida occurs when the spinal cord does not form properly and it often results in paralysis. Ireland has a high rate of spina bifida: one in every 1,000 children born in Ireland has spina bifida. Taking folic acid as a supplement for three months before and three months after conception reduces the risk of the baby developing spina bifida by up to 75% (Flood 2010a).

Maternal infections

There are certain illnesses and infections that are very dangerous for the unborn baby if the mother develops them during pregnancy. One of the most serious is rubella (German measles); if the mother contracts it during the first three months of pregnancy it can cause the child to be born blind or deaf. Some relatively benign illnesses can be very serious in pregnancy; for example, chickenpox can lead to premature birth. Toxoplasmosis is a dangerous illness caused by a parasite found in animal litter. If the mother encounters it during pregnancy, there is a high risk that the child will be born visually impaired. Toxoplasmosis is discussed further in Chapter Six.

Peri-natal factors

Peri-natal factors are factors that occur during the birth process, some of which can have an effect on the child's health. These include:

- pre-maturity
- post-term birth
- multiple births
- prolonged labour
- anoxia.

Pre-maturity

For optimum development, pregnancy should last 40 weeks. Babies born before 34 weeks are considered to be premature or pre-term. Advances in medical care mean that the survival and long-term outcomes of premature babies are better than ever. However, some difficulties will still arise, which may include the following.

- **Breathing**: a pre-term baby's respiratory system will be immature, so the child may have difficulty breathing by themselves and may need assistance.

▶ **Control of body temperature** is difficult because the baby is low weight and has little fat for insulation.

▶ **Resistance to infection** is usually low.

▶ **Jaundice** is a yellowing of the skin caused by immaturity of the liver system.

Post-term babies

Babies born after 40 weeks may experience feeding and breathing problems because the placenta will have stopped working efficiently.

Multiple births

Multiple births often result in prolonged labour and carry more risk for both mother and babies during pregnancy and birth. Multiple pregnancies will be closely monitored during pregnancy and the birth process.

Prolonged labour/anoxia

Prolonged labour leads to a higher risk of the baby becoming tired and deprived of oxygen. **Anoxia** is the term for when the baby's oxygen supply is reduced or cut off. This may be caused by a long labour, the baby being in the breech (feet first) position or the umbilical cord being squeezed. Anoxia can result in physical/intellectual disability. There have been several high-profile court cases in recent years in which parents have sought damages on behalf of children born with physical/intellectual disabilities due to anoxia caused by medical negligence.

Nutrition in childhood

Children need a balanced and nutritious diet to promote optimal health. For babies, breast milk is the best food source, providing all the nutrients the child needs as well as essential antibodies. Exclusive breastfeeding is recommended for the first six months of the child's life (DoHC 2005); however, many Irish mothers do not breastfeed for this long. As the child grows, a balanced diet based on the food pyramid is needed to promote health. Sugar and fatty foods should be limited and the intake of fruit and vegetables encouraged. Chapter Five discusses in more detail the nutritional needs of young children and how nutrition affects children's health.

Poverty

Children who live in poverty are at a higher risk of health problems than children who do not. There are degrees of poverty: absolute poverty means not having enough money to pay for food, water and shelter; relative poverty refers to households whose income is much lower than that of the general population. It is estimated that 8.7% of children in Ireland live in poverty. Research suggests that living in poverty affects children's health even before birth. Mothers from lower socio-economic groups are more likely to deliver a low birth weight baby (under 2.5kg/5.8lb) than mothers from higher socio-economic groups. Low birth weight is associated with delayed growth and cognitive development in later childhood.

Living in poverty may lead to a variety of health problems. Many studies have found that people in disadvantaged households tend to have a poorer diet than those in better-off households, and poorer families tend to be less likely to eat fruit and vegetables. As you will learn in Chapter Five, a poor diet can causes health problems as children miss out on essential nutrients. Children in poorer households may also be fed cheaper processed food, which is high in salt, sugar and calories. Poorer-quality housing may be damp, and this can lead to problems such as bronchitis and chest infections and may worsen chronic conditions such as asthma and eczema.

IDENTIFYING ILLNESS

As an ECCE worker you must have the knowledge to be able to identify when a child is unwell. Children will show both physical and psychological **signs** and **symptoms** when they are unwell. A sign is something that is easily observable (e.g. a runny nose); a symptom is something which is not readily observable (e.g. a headache).

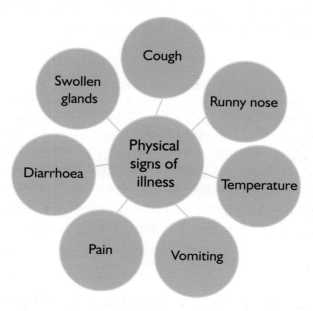

Figure 2.6 Physical signs and symptoms that a child is sick

Cough

A cough is both a symptom of disease and a protective mechanism. It is the body's natural reflex to an irritation in the throat, nose or lungs and removes excess phlegm or mucus. Coughs can also be caused by viruses. Coughs can be classified as 'wet' or 'dry'. A wet cough is 'productive' – it brings up phlegm and mucus that is clogging the respiratory system. A dry cough brings up no phlegm or mucus and is an irritant.

Treating a cough

- At night, prop the child up on pillows.
- Honey and lemon in hot water can help soothe a throat that is sore from coughing.
- If a cough persists or becomes 'chesty', consult a doctor.
- Since 2011 the Irish Medical Board has advised against the use of cough medicine for children under the age of six.

Runny nose

This happens when the nasal passage becomes congested with mucus, which sometimes leaks. A runny nose is usually a sign of a cold, but it can also be a symptom of other illnesses. The remedy for a runny nose is simply to encourage the child to blow their nose regularly to clear the nose of the mucus. Good hygiene measures should be observed: disposing of tissues and hand washing in order to limit the spread of infection.

High temperature

Normal body temperature is 36–37°C. If the child's temperature goes above this it is a sign of illness and that the child is fighting infection. A temperature of over 37.7°C in babies under six months is very serious and medical advice should always be sought. A digital or mercury thermometer will give an accurate reading of a child's body temperature. Readings can be obtained by placing the thermometer under the baby's armpit. Thermometers should not be placed in children's mouths until they are five or six years of age. Fever strips can also be used to take the child's temperature.

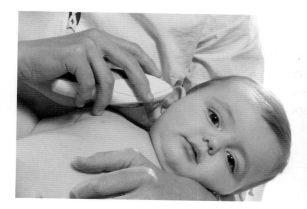
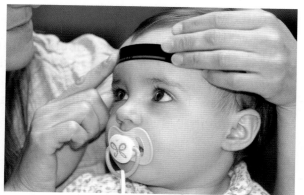

Children can develop a high temperature very quickly, and if a child has a raised temperature it needs to come down as soon as possible. The following methods can help reduce a child's temperature:

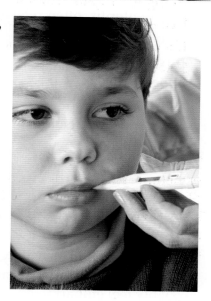

- sponging the child with a cold or tepid cloth
- opening windows to allow air to circulate in the room
- removing excess or heavy clothing, bed coverings and blankets
- encouraging the child to drink water to prevent dehydration
- parents may choose to give the child paracetamol to reduce fever.

If a child is running a high temperature that is not brought down, they are at risk of febrile convulsions, which are seizures that mostly affect children between six months and five years of age. They do not usually lead to epilepsy later in life. If a child in your care has a febrile convulsion, follow the following steps.

1 Do not attempt to hold the child down or prevent them from having the seizure.
2 Keep the child safe, and remove any obstacles that the child could injure themselves on.
3 Remove other children from the scene.
4 Call 999 or 112 and summon the ambulance service.
5 Contact the child's parents immediately.

Vomiting

This occurs when the child violently and suddenly brings up milk/food/liquid and it is a sign of illness. Vomiting can be caused by:

- posseting – bringing up small quantities of curdled milk after feeding
- excitement
- hepatitis
- concussion
- food poisoning, caused by ingesting undercooked or contaminated food or water
- gastroenteritis, often referred to as a 'tummy bug'
- whooping cough
- travel sickness
- appendicitis
- sunstroke
- a respiratory infection
- meningitis
- ear infections
- stress.

Caring for a vomiting child

Reassure the child that they will be okay. Do not blame or criticise the child for vomiting or react in a negative manner – they cannot help having vomited and probably feel embarrassed already! Get a bowl and encourage the child to vomit into this instead of on the floor. While the child is vomiting, support their head and rub their back, and continue to reassure them. When the child stops vomiting, wash their face and brush their teeth or rinse their mouth to remove the taste of vomit. Change the child's clothes and encourage them to lie down in a rest area or in bed. Keep the child hydrated by encouraging them to take sips of water. When the child begins to feel better, reintroduce foods slowly, starting with plain dry foods such as dry toast. Children should be excluded from the childcare setting for 48 hours after vomiting.

Diarrhoea

Diarrhoea is a sign of irritation in the intestines, causing the stools to be watery, loose and frequent, which may result in dehydration.

Causes

- Diarrhoea is a general symptom of infection and is specifically a symptom of gastroenteritis, or a 'tummy bug'.
- Too much dietary fibre in young children can lead to diarrhoea. This is known as toddler diarrhoea.
- Diarrhoea can be a symptom of food poisoning.

Treatment

- Diarrhoea leads to dehydration, so it is important to keep the child hydrated by offering regular drinks of water.
- Hygiene is very important to limit the spread of the infection. The child and anyone dealing with the child must wash their hands frequently. The toilet(s) used by the child must be disinfected. Any toys the child may have played with should also be disinfected in case of cross-infection.
- If a child under one year of age has diarrhoea for more than six hours they should be taken to the medical services as they can easily dehydrate. Children experiencing diarrhoea should be excluded from the ECCE setting until 48 hours from onset.

Pain

Pain is the body's warning sign that something is wrong and is a response to an injury or distress in the affected area. Older children will be able to tell you if they are in pain, but very young children may not have the vocabulary to do this. They will, however, show non-verbal signs that they are in pain, for example:

- pulling at and rubbing the ear
- holding the tummy
- moving awkwardly.

In babies, signs include:

- squeezing the eyes shut
- pulling the mouth taut
- squeezing the eyebrows together to make a bulge of flesh between the eyebrows.

Earache

A pain in the ear is usually caused by an ear infection, but it can be a symptom of another illness such as tonsillitis or mumps. If pain is severe and the child has a fever, call the doctor straight away.

Headache

A headache is often a symptom of illness. One in five children suffer from recurrent headaches, although these are usually not serious (Stoppard 2006). Headaches are often caused by being in a warm, stuffy room, but they can also be caused by:

- sinusitis
- toothache
- a blow to the head
- meningitis
- raised temperature
- earache
- allergies.

Swollen glands/lymph nodes

The lymph nodes produce white blood cells, which the body uses to fight infection. Lymph nodes are positioned in the neck, armpit and groin. Swollen glands are caused by a build-up of white blood cells.

Psychological signs and symptoms

Illness in children produces psychological effects as well as physical signs. The following are signs that something is 'not right' with a child and may, in combination with physical signs, be an indication of illness.

Figure 2.7 Psychological signs of illness

Regressive behaviour

We say a child is exhibiting 'regressive behaviour' if they start to act in a way that is more suited to an earlier stage of development. For example, children in hospital often look for a comfort blanket that they had outgrown, or want to play with toys suitable for a younger child. Regressive behaviour is often a sign that something is 'not quite right' with a child.

No interest in toys

A child showing a lack of interest in a previously loved toy can be a sign of illness. Similarly, a child may have no interest in activities, toys or stories of any kind.

Changes in behaviour

Sudden changes in behaviour can be sign of illness. For example, a usually placid child may become irritable and cranky and a usually difficult child may become withdrawn.

Irritableness

When a child (or adult!) is feeling under the weather they may feel cranky and be irritable. An irritable mood is often (but not always) a sign of illness.

Attention seeking/clinginess

Very young children may seek a parent's attention when they are sick in order to get comfort. This can be shown in attention-seeking behaviour such as crying, clinginess, etc.

VACCINATION

Immunisation is a key factor in promoting children's health. Immunisation protects children against serious viruses. We become immune to a disease when we contract it and our body makes white blood cells to fight against it. The white blood cells create antibodies which fight the infection. Vaccinations contain very small parts of viruses, which are treated so that they won't cause disease but will activate the body's defence system. The body creates antibodies to fight the infection and thus gains immunity against the disease. There are two types of immunity: **passive immunity** and **active immunity**.

Passive immunity occurs when we take in antibodies from someone else to gain immunity against illness. For example, babies who are breastfed receive antibodies from their mother in breast milk. As long as they are breastfed, the baby will be immune to whatever illnesses the mother is immune to.

Active immunity occurs when we make the white blood cell antibodies ourselves, which happens when our body encounters an infection. We make white blood cells to fight against the infection, which remain in our bloodstream and give immunity against that illness for life.

Table 2.2 Current vaccination schedule in Ireland (as of September 2008)

When	Where	What
Birth	Hospital/clinic	BCG
2 months	GP	6 in 1 + PCV
4 months	GP	6 in 1 + meningitis C
6 months	GP	6 in 1 + meningitis C + PCV
12 months	GP	MMR + PCV
13 months	GP	Meningitis C + Hib
4–5 years	GP/school	4 in 1 + MMR
1st year in secondary school	School	HPV
6th year in secondary school	School	HPV
11–14 years	School	Tdap

Source: National Immunisation Office 2011

What are the vaccinations?

- **BCG:** vaccination against tuberculosis.
- **6 in 1:** vaccination against polio, diphtheria, *Haemophilus influenzae* type B (Hib), whooping cough, tetanus, hepatitis B.
- **4 in 1:** diphtheria, whooping cough, tetanus, polio.

- **MMR:** measles, mumps, rubella.
- **HPV:** human papillomavirus.
- **PCV:** pneumococcal vaccine.
- **Tdap:** tetanus, diphtheria and whooping cough.
- **MenC:** meningococcal C.

Possible reactions to vaccination

Minor reactions include:

- redness/soreness in the area where the vaccination was given
- slight fever
- headache.

Some more severe reactions include:

- dizziness
- swelling in the area where the vaccination was given
- wheezing
- hoarseness.

CASE STUDY: THE MMR VACCINATION AND AUTISM

In 1995 an article published in the prestigious medical journal *The Lancet* claimed that there was a link between the MMR vaccination and cases of autism in children. The paper's main author, Andrew Wakefield, discussed 12 cases of children whom he claimed had been developing as normal until receiving the MMR vaccine and then began to exhibit signs and symptoms of autism. The study caused a huge media controversy and resulted in a dip in parents choosing to have their children vaccinated.

At the same time, the scientific community was picking holes in the methodology of Wakefield's study. First, Wakefield used a very small sample: most scientific research uses samples of hundreds of participants, and 12 participants is simply too small a sample size on which to base the kind of claims that Wakefield was making. Second, the study used retrospective interviews to support its claims: Wakefield asked parents about their children's behaviour before the vaccine many years after it had been administered. This is not considered good practice – our memory is not always completely accurate when recalling events in the past.

Many studies were conducted that rectified some of the flaws in Wakefield's methodology. None of the studies using large samples of children found a link between autism and the MMR vaccine.

In 2010 Wakefield was struck off by the British Medical Council for deliberately falsifying data and altering his results. The link between the MMR vaccine and autism has been discredited and the original article withdrawn.

Signpost for reflection

How do you promote children's health in your role as an ECCE worker? How could you further develop your role as a health educator and health promoter?

chapter three

Common Childhood Illnesses

After reading this chapter you will:

- be able to identify the signs and symptoms of common childhood illness
- be familiar with the treatment for a range of common childhood illnesses
- be able to define what is meant by a chronic condition
- be familiar with a range of chronic conditions
- have an awareness of issues affecting the care of children in hospital.

This chapter continues the theme of Chapter Two and discusses in some detail some common childhood illnesses you may encounter in your work with young children. For the purposes of this chapter, illnesses are divided into the following categories:

- illnesses in babies
- digestive problems
- infections of the ear and eye
- urinary tract infections
- viruses
- chronic conditions
- skin disorders.

ILLNESSES IN BABIES

In this section we will look at croup and bronchiolitis.

Croup

Croup is a common disorder affecting children aged from six months to three years. It is an inflammation and narrowing of the trachea caused by a viral infection. Croup occurs more often in the autumn and winter months.

Signs and symptoms

Early symptoms include a runny nose and cold-like symptoms. This develops into a barking cough and wheezing when breathing, accompanied by breathlessness. In severe cases breathing becomes difficult, resulting in a shortage of oxygen.

Treatment

The GP may prescribe medication to ease breathing difficulties. Exposure to night air can also be helpful, as can sitting in a steamy bathroom. In severe cases hospitalisation may be required.

Bronchiolitis

Bronchiolitis is an inflammation of the airways in the lungs, which is caused by a viral infection. It is common in and usually only affects babies under 12 months.

Signs and symptoms

- Cough.
- Rapid breathing.
- Wheezing.
- Feeding difficulties.

> **IF A CHILD UNDER ONE YEAR DEVELOPS THESE SYMPTOMS, CONTACT THE DOCTOR IMMEDIATELY!**

Treatment

The GP will prescribe an inhaler to relieve the airways; in severe cases hospitalisation may be required.

DIGESTIVE PROBLEMS

The following problems are related to digestive illness in young children:

- appendicitis
- constipation
- gastroenteritis
- threadworms.

Appendicitis

The appendix is a part of the small intestine. Appendicitis occurs when the appendix becomes partly or wholly blocked, resulting in infection and inflammation. When this happens the appendix may need to be surgically removed (an appendectomy). Appendicitis is a common occurrence in young children but is rare in babies under a year.

Cause

There is no known cause of appendicitis.

Signs and symptoms

The main symptom of appendicitis is an acute abdominal pain, starting in the navel, moving down to the lower right side. This is accompanied by a slightly raised temperature, loss of appetite and possibly vomiting, diarrhoea or constipation.

Treatment

Appendicitis should be suspected if a child complains of abdominal pain for more than a few hours. Lie the child on their back and gently press the stomach on the right-hand side. If the child experiences pain from this gentle pressure and sharp pain when you remove your hand, appendicitis should be suspected and medical treatment should be sought immediately.

Constipation

Constipation occurs when the child has difficulty passing stools or passes stools that are hard and pebble-like. Occasional constipation is not serious, but chronic constipation can cause problems later in life.

Causes

Constipation is usually caused by a diet that does not contain enough fibre and fluid. You will learn more about fibre in Chapter Five.

Signs and symptoms

- The child passes hard, pebble-like stools.
- Pain in the lower abdomen.
- Blood on the nappy or underpants: this is a sign that the child is straining to pass stools.

Treatment

> Parents should consult their GP for advice.
> Include natural, unprocessed foods in the child's diet and reduce processed foods.
> Increase the child's fluid intake.

Gastroenteritis

Gastroenteritis (also known as tummy bug) is an inflammation of the stomach and intestines.

Causes

Gastroenteritis is most commonly passed on as a viral infection, usually by a rotavirus or astrovirus, which are inhaled, and it can spread quickly through a community. It can also be caused by food poisoning.

Signs and symptoms

> Vomiting.
> Nausea.
> Diarrhoea.
> Abdominal cramps.
> Loss of appetite.
> Raised temperature.

Treatment

> Stop all foods and milk.
> Keep the child hydrated.
> Notify the parents and ask them to collect the child. The child will not be able to return to the ECCE setting until 48 hours after they last vomited/had diarrhoea.
> Hygiene is important in limiting the spread of the infection; make sure the child washes their hand and wash down any contaminated surfaces with disinfectant.

Threadworms

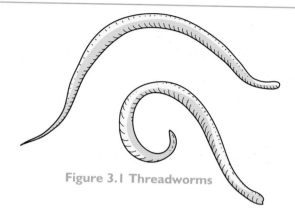

Figure 3.1 Threadworms

Threadworms (also known as worms) are minute parasites that look like very fine threads of white cotton and measure up to one centimetre in length. Infestations of threadworms are very common in children, especially those aged 5–9 years.

Causes

Threadworm eggs are invisible to the naked eye and are found on skin, dust, clothes and toys. Children catch threadworms by ingesting the eggs. This usually happens when the child sucks on an object or eats food that has been contaminated with the eggs. These eggs will develop into adult worms in the intestine. The worms lay their eggs on the skin surrounding the anus. The resultant itching causes the child to scratch their bottom. The eggs remain under the fingernails unless they are killed by hand washing. If the child puts their hand in their mouth after scratching they will ingest the new eggs and the cycle begins again.

Signs and symptoms

- Itching in the anal area, especially at night.
- Inflammation and redness in the anus as a result of scratching.
- The worms can sometimes be seen as thin white threads in the child's faeces.

Treatment

Over-the-counter medication can be obtained from the chemist and should be administered to the entire family. Once the drugs have been administered all bedclothes should be changed and the old bedclothes washed in hot water to kill any residual eggs. Vacuum children's play areas and bathrooms to kill any residual eggs and disinfect the toilet area regularly. Children should be discouraged from scratching their bottom as this perpetrates the cycle of infection. Exclusion from the ECCE setting is not necessary.

INFECTIONS OF THE EAR AND EYE

Ear infections

Ear infections, which are common in young children, may be located in the outer ear (otitis externa) or middle ear (otitis media). Otitis externa is usually caused by a foreign object or a boil, or by scratching and damaging the outer ear. Otitis media is usually caused by a build-up of fluid in the middle ear. One in five children under the age of four have an ear infection at least once a year.

Signs and symptoms

- Pain in the ear.
- Raised temperature.
- Ears crackle, pop, feel tight.
- You may be able to see a boil or foreign object in the ear.
- Difficulty hearing.

Treatment and care

- Medical advice must be sought.
- Paracetamol may be given – on a doctor's advice – to ease the pain.
- Ice packs may help ease inflammation.

Glue ear

Glue ear is the name given to partial deafness which can occur in young children. The hearing loss fluctuates; sometimes the child will appear to have good hearing, at other times very little hearing. Hearing loss as a result of glue ear is temporary and should not permanently affect the child.

Causes

Glue ear is caused by a build-up of fluid in the middle ear. This is usually as a result of repeated infections, which block the ear so that fluid cannot drain out. This build-up of fluid causes deafness.

Signs and symptoms

◗ Partial deafness.

◗ Speech development may be affected.

◗ Poor performance in school can result as the child may miss out on information.

◗ Behavioural changes may result from the frustration of not being able to hear.

◗ Difficulty concentrating.

Treatment and care

If it is suspected that a child may have glue ear, medical advice must be sought. The GP may prescribe antibiotics to treat the infection, but if the child has repeated cases of glue ear the GP may refer the child to an ear, nose and throat (ENT) specialist, who may choose to surgically insert grommets. These are tiny plastic tubes which allow the mucus and fluid to drain away.

Conjunctivitis

Conjunctivitis (also known as pink eye) is an inflammation of the membrane covering the eyeball and inside of the eyelid, causing the eye to become red and weepy. It can affect one or both eyes and is contagious.

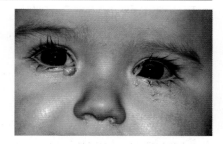

Causes

Conjunctivitis can be caused by a bacterial or viral infection, by a foreign body in the eye or by chemicals. It can also be the result of an allergic reaction.

Signs and symptoms

◗ Red, weepy eye.

◗ Painful eye.

◗ Eye becomes very itchy.

◗ Eye is irritated by bright light.

Treatment

Conjunctivitis is easily treated by eye drops prescribed by the child's GP. Bathing the eye may also be useful. As conjunctivitis is contagious, hygiene measures must be implemented and the child should be taught not to rub their eye. Children with conjunctivitis may be excluded from the ECCE setting until 48 hours after starting a course of antibiotics (HSE 2012a).

URINARY TRACT INFECTIONS

A urinary tract infection (UTI) is the name given to an infection in any part of the urinary tract and may affect the kidney, bladder or urethra. UTIs are more common in girls than boys: 11% of girls and 4% of boys experience a UTI before the age of 16 (HSE 2012b).

Causes

The main cause of UTIs is bacteria being spread from the rectum to the urethra, usually as a result of wiping back to front after using the toilet. UTIs may also be caused by constipation or as a result of 'holding on' to urine for too long, despite a need to urinate.

Signs and symptoms

- Fever.
- Diarrhoea.
- Vomiting.
- Strong-smelling urine.

In older children symptoms may also include:

- a burning sensation while urinating
- a frequent urge to urinate
- bedwetting
- cloudy urine
- lower back or abdominal pain.

Treatment

The child will need to see their GP, who will take a sample of urine to test for a UTI. If an infection is present the GP will prescribe a course of antibiotics. The child should drink plenty of fluids and empty their bladder regularly. Children should be taught to wipe from front to back after using the toilet to minimise the risk of UTIs.

VIRUSES

Viral infections involve many parts of the body and include some very serious diseases. This section will discuss the following viruses:

- chickenpox
- mumps
- measles
- rubella
- meningitis and septicaemia
- influenza
- hand, foot and mouth disease
- tuberculosis (TB)
- scarlet fever.

Chickenpox

Chickenpox is a common childhood illness, and is sometimes seen as a rite of passage for young children. It is usually not serious, but it can be serious in children with HIV or children who are taking medicine for childhood cancer. Chickenpox is more serious if contracted in adulthood.

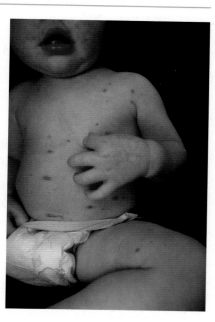

Causes

Chickenpox is an airborne viral infection caused by the varicella-zoster virus (VZC). It is spread by inhaling the coughs and sneezes of those infected with the virus.

Signs and symptoms

- Mild fever or headache.
- A rash with small red pimples, which begins on the chest and back. This spreads to the face, scalp and arms, turning into an itchy outbreak of blisters.
- The rash is accompanied by intense itching.

Treatment

If you suspect that a child in your care has chickenpox, first reassure the child, then contact the parents and ask them to remove the child from the setting and take the child to the doctor. The child will not be able to return to the setting until five to seven days after the rash disappears (HSE 2012a). Parents of other children will have to be notified that there has been a case of chickenpox in the setting, and this is best done by letter (see the sample letter in Appendix I). The infected child's name must not be mentioned in the letter.

There is no antibiotic for children with chickenpox; the only treatment is rest and to dress the child in loose, non-itchy clothing. Bathing in camomile lotion can help to soothe the itchy rash.

Mumps

Mumps is a viral infection that causes fever and swelling of the glands around the neck. Mumps is preventable by administration of the MMR vaccination.

Causes

Mumps is spread in saliva and air droplets in coughs and sneezes.

Signs and symptoms

▶ Swelling of the glands on either side of the face just below the ears and beneath the chin.
▶ Boys may experience swollen, painful testes and girls may experience lower abdominal pain.
▶ Pain when swallowing.
▶ The child may experience headache and fever.

Treatment

A hot water bottle wrapped in a towel can help to soothe the affected area and paracetamol may help to reduce pain. Soft, liquid food should be given. Children who present with mumps should be excluded from the ECCE setting until five days after the swelling begins (HSE 2012a). Parents of other children attending the setting will have to be notified that there has been a case of mumps in the setting.

Possible complications

In rare cases mumps can cause infertility in boys due to swelling of the testes.

Measles

Measles is a viral infection that results in a non-itchy rash. Measles can lead to serious complications, such as meningitis and encephalitis, which can cause brain damage. Because of this, measles is vaccinated against in the MMR vaccine. Measles is an extremely serious disease, which kills approximately one million children annually.

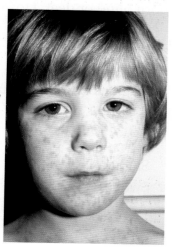

Causes

Measles is a viral, airborne infection.

Signs and symptoms

- The child will seem generally unwell and may have a high temperature and fever.
- A flat blotchy rash starting behind the ears and spreading over the torso.
- Grey spots on the inside of the gum (known as Koplik's spots).
- The child may develop small white spots inside the mouth.
- The eyes may be red and sore and intolerant to light.
- Runny nose and a hacking cough.

Treatment

- Keep the child comfortable and encourage them to rest.
- If the child's eyes are affected you may need to keep the child in a slightly darkened room.

Children with measles should be excluded from the ECCE setting for five days after the rash appears (HSE 2012a). Parents of other children attending the setting must be informed.

Rubella

Rubella is also known as German measles. It is a fairly mild illness, but it can have very serious side effects if contracted by a pregnant woman. If a woman in the early stages of pregnancy contracts rubella there is a strong likelihood that her child will be born blind or deaf. However, the MMR vaccination has virtually eliminated rubella.

Causes

Rubella is an airborne viral infection spread in droplets in the air. Carriers are contagious for one day before and four days after the rash appears.

Signs and symptoms

▶ Slight fever.
▶ Swollen glands in the back of the neck and behind the ears.
▶ A non-itchy rash of tiny pink spots.

Treatment

There is no antibiotic for rubella and the child will recover with rest. Children with rubella should be excluded from the ECCE setting for seven days after the rash appears. Any staff members who are pregnant or may be pregnant should see their doctor. Parents of children who attend the setting should also be encouraged to seek medical advice.

Meningitis

Meningitis is a serious, potentially life-threatening infection of the brain and the covering of the spinal cord.

Causes

Meningitis can be caused by a viral or bacterial infection. Bacterial meningitis is usually more serious than viral meningitis. Bacterial meningitis is caused by *Haemophilus influenzae* type B (Hib) or meningococcal type C (MenC). A vaccination is available for both Hib and MenC.

Signs and symptoms

In infants:

- high-pitched cry
- poor feeding
- difficulty walking
- bulging of the soft spot in the head.

In older children:

- fever
- vomiting
- stiff neck
- sensitivity to light
- severe fatigue
- signs of cold and flu
- a rash that doesn't disappear under pressure (the glass test)
- a temperature.

The rash that is associated with meningitis is actually a sign of **septicaemia** or blood poisoning. This occurs when bacteria release toxins into the blood, damaging the blood vessel walls, which allows blood to leak out, causing a rash. The main sign of septicaemia is a rash that does not disappear under pressure (the glass test).

Treatment

Meningitis is a potentially fatal condition. If a child in your care exhibits any of the signs of meningitis, emergency medical care should be sought at once. Parents of other children attending the setting will have to be informed of the case.

Influenza

Influenza is a viral infection affecting the lungs, throat and bronchi that usually lasts a week. There are many different strains of the flu virus, so a child may be immune to one strain but not immune to another. Influenza is a severe illness, especially for the very old and very young.

Signs and symptoms

▶ High fever.
▶ Aching muscles.
▶ Headache.
▶ Cough.
▶ Sore throat.
▶ Runny nose.

Treatment

Children who have influenza should be excluded from ECCE settings for one week from when their symptoms begin. An influenza injection is available each winter for elderly people and for those with an underlying condition such as asthma.

Hand, foot and mouth disease:

Hand, foot and mouth disease is a viral infection common in children under the age of four. It causes small blisters in the mouth and on the hands and feet.

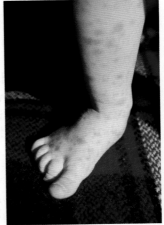

Symptoms

▶ Blisters inside the mouth which may develop into painful ulcers.
▶ Blisters on the hand and feet, developing one to two days after the blisters in the mouth.
▶ Fever.
▶ Children may be reluctant to eat if mouth ulcers develop.

Treatment

The virus should only last a few days. During this time ensure that the child has plenty to drink and stays hydrated. Avoid fruit juices as they may irritate mouth ulcers. Paracetamol is useful to control temperature. The child should be excluded from the setting until the blisters disappear from their hands.

Tuberculosis

Tuberculosis (TB) is a bacterial infection affecting the lungs. In the past TB was a major cause of death and disability in Ireland. Vaccinations have all but eliminated TB, but a dip in uptake means that there has been somewhat of a resurgence of TB in recent years. To combat this, the BCG vaccination, which protects against TB, is once again part of the nationwide vaccination schedule.

Signs and symptoms

- The first sign of TB is a cough which becomes persistent.
- Chest pain when inhaling deeply.
- Shortness of breath.
- Fever.
- Poor appetite and weight loss.
- Sweating at night.
- Tiredness.
- Coughing up green or yellow sputum, which may be streaked with blood.

TB can be diagnosed with a chest X-ray or a computerised tomography (CT) scan for lung damage.

Treatment

TB is treated with anti-tuberculosis drugs for at least six months. These can usually be administered at home unless the child is very ill. TB is a notifiable disease and the child will have to be excluded from the setting until they are no longer infectious. All those in contact with the child will have to be screened for TB.

Scarlet fever

Scarlet fever is an infection that causes a widespread scarlet rash and sore throat. Scarlet fever was a dangerous childhood disease until the introduction of antibiotics.

Signs and symptoms

- Sore throat and headache.
- Fever and vomiting.
- Scarlet rash on neck, arms, chest and groin.
- Tongue may be covered in a white coating: this will disappear in a few days, leaving the tongue bright red.

Treatment

The GP will prescribe an antibiotic, which will treat the infection rapidly, with symptoms beginning to improve within 24–48 hours. Children can return to the setting once they have been on antibiotics for 24 hours and feel well enough to return.

CHRONIC CONDITIONS

A chronic condition is a long-lasting condition that cannot be cured – but can be managed – and lasts or is expected to last more than three months. Examples of chronic conditions include cystic fibrosis, asthma, diabetes, eczema and any long-term medical condition.

A chronic illness can potentially affect a child physically, intellectually, socially and emotionally.

- **Physical effects:** The child may experience delayed growth and developmental delay, especially if they are hospitalised for long periods of time. In the case of some chronic illnesses, such as cystic fibrosis, the child may be at risk of a nutritional deficiency. A nutritionist may be assigned to help balance the child's diet.
- **Intellectual effects:** If the child is in and out of hospital frequently they may miss schooling, leading to delayed development of literacy and numeracy skills. Disrupted education may also lead to the child falling behind in school. Children's hospitals such as Temple Street do provide teachers and education for patients; however, attendance is dependent on the child's health.
- **Social and emotional effects:** Because of frequent absences from school the child may have lower confidence in making and sustaining friendships. Parents may be over-protective of children and this may lead to delayed development of independent living skills. Emotional development may be delayed, leading to regressive behaviour, behaviour problems and poor self esteem.

Chronic illness will also affect the child's parents. The strain of looking after a child with chronic illness can lead to physical and mental exhaustion, especially if the child is hospitalised frequently or for long periods. Parents naturally want to protect their children, but they cannot control the effects of the illness. This may lead to feelings of anxiety, loss of control, fear, guilt, helplessness and isolation. Finally, the medical costs associated with dealing with a chronic illness may be high, and there is a risk that parents can get into financial difficulties.

The child's siblings will also be affected in a complex way. They may feel increased responsibility and a need to protect and look after their sibling. They will be naturally concerned and worried about their sibling's well-being. At the same time, they may experience feelings of jealousy that the sibling is getting all the parents' attention and they may seek attention, sometimes through negative behaviour. These conflicting emotions can leave the child feeling guilty and embarrassed.

My Sister's Keeper by Jodi Picoult, which was also adapted into a film, describes the effects of a child's chronic illness (leukaemia) on her family, in particular her older brother and younger sister. The book and film chart the journey of the family as each member deals with the illness in their own way.

If you are caring for a child with chronic illness in an ECCE setting, the following steps should be taken.

- The key worker system is vital to help the child to feel secure in the setting.
- Allow the child to express their feelings, and provide activities that can help them release tensions and frustration.
- Always find time to listen to the child.
- Support the family.

Asthma

Asthma is a chronic condition that affects breathing. It causes the airways to become oversensitive to triggers such as dust, which makes the airways go into spasm, making breathing difficult. This spasm is known as an asthma attack. Ireland has the fourth highest rate of asthma in the world (Asthma Society of Ireland website), and a recent survey found that 5.8% of three-year-olds have had a diagnosis of asthma (ESRI and Trinity College Dublin: *Growing Up in Ireland* 2011). It is not known exactly what causes asthma, but possible causes are thought to include:

- increased pollution in the environment
- low birth weight
- smoking in pregnancy
- children spending more time indoors.

There are certain substances that act as a 'triggers' and can bring on an asthma attack. Different children will have different triggers, but known triggers include:

- dust mites
- pollen
- certain foods

- coughs and colds
- exercise
- stress
- humidity
- mould
- changes in the weather.

Children with asthma should carry an inhaler to be used in the event of an asthma attack. There are two types of inhaler: preventers and relievers. Preventer inhalers are brown and are used to prevent asthma attacks. Reliever inhalers are blue and are to be administered to the child if they have an asthma attack. The reliever inhaler will ease the airways and make breathing easier.

If you are caring for a child with asthma you will have to know how to deal with an asthma attack. Parents will provide guidance, but here are some general pointers.

- Reassure the child.
- Give the child their inhaler – young children may use a spacer.
- Send for help.
- Sit the child upright and leaning forward.
- Document the attack and inform the child's parents.

Although children sometimes grow out of asthma, it is a chronic condition that cannot be cured. However, steps can be taken to reduce the likelihood of an attack. The following are some guidelines on how to do this.

- Vacuum mattress, pillow and base of bed.
- Use quilts and duvets with synthetic fillings, not feathers.
- Damp dust the skirting boards, windowsills and floors every week.
- Wash bedroom soft fittings every week.

CASE STUDY: A CHILD WITH ASTHMA

Alice had repeated chest infections as a baby, resulting in hospitalisation on two occasions. She had frequent episodes of wheezing and coughing. Alice's GP prescribed inhalers but a definitive diagnosis of asthma was not made until Alice was six. Alice now uses both a preventer and a reliever inhaler. Her mother administers the preventer inhaler every morning in order to help keep the airways clear. Alice carries the reliever inhaler with her in case she starts to have an asthma attack when she is out and about.

When Alice was younger her mother administered her inhalers using a spacer, but now Alice is beginning to take responsibility for her condition. She has learned to identify the signs that she needs a 'puff' – tightening of the chest, shortness of breath – and then takes the inhaler, under adult supervision. Some things make Alice's asthma worse. She can feel worse when the seasons change in spring and autumn, and in summer if the pollen count is high. Dust mites worsen Alice's asthma, so her parents make sure to keep the house dust free, vacuuming at least three times a week and washing her bedding once a week. They got rid of the heavy carpets in the house and keep soft toys to a minimum. Alice recently joined the under eight football team. Her parents make sure to give her the preventer inhaler before training and stay for the session in case she needs a reliever inhaler.

Diabetes

Diabetes occurs when the body is unable to regulate the amount of sugar in the bloodstream. This may be because the body is not producing sufficient amounts of insulin, a chemical that regulates blood sugar level, or because the body is not processing insulin effectively.

There are two types of diabetes: **type I** diabetes is caused by genetic factors and occurs when the pancreas does not produce insulin; **type II** diabetes is usually associated with being overweight. In the past, type II diabetes was rare in children, but with the rise of childhood obesity it is becoming more common.

Treatment

Diabetes is treated by a combination of diet and medication. Children who are diabetic will have to follow a reduced sugar diet (explained in more detail in Chapter Five). Some children will also need insulin, which they will have to take before meals. Insulin is injected and as children get older they will be able to administer this themselves, but if you are caring for a young child with diabetes you will have to administer the insulin for them. Parents will advise and provide training on how to do this.

Hypoglycaemia and hyperglycaemia

If you are caring for a child with diabetes you will have to be vigilant in looking out for hypoglycaemia and hyperglycaemia. These conditions occur when the person with diabetes does not regulate their blood sugar properly by missing meals or injecting too much insulin.

Hypoglycaemia is caused by low blood sugar, usually resulting from skipping meals or not eating enough. If the child has a hypoglycaemic attack (sometimes called a hypo) they will feel:

- shaky and weak
- lightheaded
- sleepy and dizzy
- nervous and anxious
- grouchy
- confused.

If the child is hypoglycaemic they need sugar quickly to stabilise their blood sugar levels. Give the child a third to half a glass of a sugary drink such as Lucozade or 7-Up or 200ml of fruit juice or two teaspoons of sugar. If symptoms do not improve within 10–15 minutes, repeat the treatment. Parents should always be informed if their child has had a 'hypo'.

Note: If the child engages in unexpected physical activity they will need to take in extra food to prevent a 'hypo'.

Hyperglycaemia is caused by too much sugar in the bloodstream, usually caused by missing an insulin injection. Hyperglycaemia is potentially life-threatening. Symptoms include the following:

- looking flushed
- feeling unwell
- feeling grumpy
- going to the toilet a lot
- lack of energy.

If the child appears to be experiencing high blood sugar levels, notify the parents.

Note: The Diabetes Federation of Ireland has produced a children's explanatory booklet about diabetes, called *Pete the Pancreas.*

Epilepsy

Epilepsy is a neurological condition, which means that it affects the activity of the brain. Epilepsy causes seizures, when normal brain activity is interrupted. The seizure may be **generalised** and affect all the brain, causing the person to lose consciousness, or it may be **partial**. The person may remain conscious during a partial seizure, although consciousness may be impaired in some way. According to Brainwave, the Irish Epilepsy Association, epilepsy affects one in every 115 people (Brainwave website).

A **tonic-clonic seizure**, sometimes called a 'grand mal' seizure, is an example of a generalised seizure affecting the whole brain. The tonic-clonic seizure is made up of four stages:

1. The **aura** is the onset of the seizure, when some people see lights or smell particular scents.
2. In the **tonic** phase the person's entire body stiffens and they fall to the floor, losing consciousness. The back and neck may arc, with the arms flexed and hands clenched.
3. In the **clonic** stage the body will begin to twitch, jerk and spasm.
4. In the **post-convulsive stage** the person will remain unconscious for a short period of time.

An **absence**, sometimes called a 'petit mal', affects the whole brain. During an absence the child is momentarily unaware of what is going on around him or her but quickly returns to consciousness. To the observer it may seem as if the child is experiencing a short staring spell.

Treatment

Anti-epileptic medication will be prescribed to attempt to control seizures. This is effective in 70% of cases (Brainwave website). If a child in your care has an epileptic seizure, stay calm and remove any other children from the scene. Do not attempt to hold the child down or prevent them from having the seizure. Remove any obstacles that could injure the child. If it is the first time the child has had a seizure, call the emergency services. If the child has a history of epilepsy, medical treatment may not be necessary, but the parents must be informed.

SKIN DISORDERS

Eczema

Eczema is the name given to a group of skin complaints that occur in response to an inflammation. Atopic eczema usually begins between 18 months and two years. The skin becomes itchy, dry, flaky, red and painful. Eczema commonly presents on the skin creases of elbows, wrists and behind the knees. Babies may develop eczema on the face. Eczema is often triggered by stress or by certain substances, which can include:

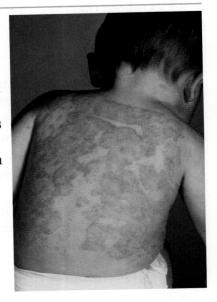

- dairy products
- eggs
- wool
- fur.

Note: different children will have different triggers for eczema.

Care

- The child must be discouraged from scratching, as this makes the rash worse. To try to limit scratching, nails should be kept short.
- Dress the child in loose cotton clothes which will not aggravate the condition.
- Over-warm rooms can aggravate the condition.
- Special soaps will have to be used.
- Anti-histamine cream will be prescribed by the doctor and used to ease the eczema.

Impetigo

Impetigo is a bacterial skin infection spread by direct contact with broken infected skin. Impetigo presents as a red blistering rash around the nose and mouth. The rash then crusts over to a honey colour.

Treatment

Impetigo is treated by antibacterial soaps and cream as well as oral antibiotics. The child should not attend the setting until treatment has begun.

CASE STUDY: A CHILD WITH ECZEMA

Mike is four years old and attends Little Tots Day Care full time, five days a week. When Mike was a baby his skin was very dry and often flared up into dry red itchy patches. He was diagnosed with eczema when he was two years old. His eczema flares up from time to time, causing patches of red, inflamed, dry, itchy skin on his arms and legs. Certain triggers seem to worsen Mike's eczema. If the house is very hot and humid this makes his eczema worse, so the temperature of the house is controlled and kept at a suitable temperature by a thermostat. Dairy products also affect Mike's eczema, so his parents try to limit the amount he eats and use substitutes such as goat's milk.

When Mike went to pre-school his parents met with Joe, his key worker, and explained about Mike's eczema and his special diet. Joe was supportive and with his co-workers has arranged to follow Mike's diet in the setting. Perfumed soaps and washing powders irritate Mike's eczema, so special soaps for sensitive skin are used at home and in the setting. Mike's skin gets dry after bathing so his parents apply emollient creams in order to lock in moisture. Sometimes Mike's eczema gets particularly itchy, causing him to scratch. To prevent this, his parents keep his nails short and during particularly bad flare-ups he wears gloves to bed.

In the setting, messy play activities like playdough, water play and gloop can exacerbate Mike's eczema. After discussion with Mike's parents it was decided to provide Mike with gloves to wear during these activities, enabling him to join in fully with the fun. Mike's parents have given Joe permission to apply emollient cream during the day if necessary, and when Mike is on steroid cream they have given Joe permission to apply this in line with the GP's instructions. Joe is happy to assist in this and has devised a record of care plan, which he marks off when the cream is administered. There are two copies of the care plan: one goes home in Mike's record of care book; the other is kept on site.

Ringworm

Ringworm is a fungal infection involving the skin, groin and feet. Ringworm presents as rough scaly circular rash. It is spread by contact with infected skin flakes or by using infected combs and brushes.

Treatment

A combination of antifungal ointments and antibiotics will be used to treat ringworm. Children do not need to be excluded from the setting, but they should be encouraged to wash their hands and use good hygiene measures to prevent the spread of infection.

Scabies

Scabies is an itchy rash caused by an infestation of the mite *Sarcoptes scabiei*, which burrows under the skin to lay its eggs. This causes intense itching. In some cases the child scratches so much that the skin is broken.

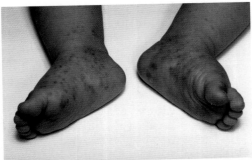

Treatment

A scabies infection can be treated with a lotion bought over the counter in the chemist. The lotion will need to be applied to every member of the household and reapplied again 4–7 days later. Bed linen and clothing will have to be changed and washed at a high temperature to kill any remaining mites. Children will not have to be excluded from the setting once they have been treated, but other parents must be informed so that they can treat their children.

Head lice

Head lice are small grey/brown insects, no bigger than 3mm in length, or about the size of a pinhead. Head lice infestations are very common and most children will encounter head lice at some stage. They affect more girls than boys, probably because girls more often share combs, hats and other items (Casey & Phelan 2008). It is not known how many Irish children are affected by head lice, but it is estimated to be 8% of primary school children every year (Casey & Phelan 2008).

Figure 3.2 Head louse

The head louse hatches from a white shell, which remains stuck to the hair shaft after the louse hatches. This shells are known as 'nits'. The shell grows with the shaft of hair and the date of infestation can be estimated by determining the distance from the scalp to the shell furthest from it. A female louse lives for 25–30 days and can lay six to eight eggs daily, each of which will hatch after seven or eight days. Contrary to popular belief, head lice do not fly or jump from one head to another. They spread through head to head contact, from sharing hair accessories and hair brushes.

Signs and symptoms

- The scalp will be itchy, particularly at the nape of the neck and behind the ears.
- Nits may be visible.
- Lice shed their skin at night and leave a black dust-like deposit on pillowcases.

Head lice myths

1 Head lice do not prefer clean hair to dirty hair – they can be found on both!
2 Although head lice are more common in children, anyone can get head lice.
3 Head lice cannot jump or fly; they spread through head to head contact.
4 You cannot catch head lice from pets.
5 While itching is often a sign of head lice, not everyone with head lice will have an itchy scalp.
6 Head lice do not prefer long hair to short hair.

Treatment

- Prevention is better than cure and parents should regularly check their children's hair for signs of lice.
- Many medicated shampoos that kill lice are available over the counter. These should only be used if lice are present in hair as overuse reduces its effectiveness.
- Nits are difficult to remove; they stick to the hair shaft and can only be removed by combing wet hair with a fine tooth comb.
- Washing children's hair using tea tree shampoo can prevent lice from recurring.
- Encourage children with long hair to tie it back.
- Any clothing or bed linen that may have been infested must be washed in hot water to sterilise it.
- Brushes and combs should be boiled for ten minutes or soaked in dilute bleach for an hour in order to kill any residual lice or unhatched eggs.

Head lice in an ECCE setting

Many ECCE settings will experience an outbreak of head lice at one stage or another. If an outbreak occurs you must write to all parents informing them of the outbreak and outlining treatment steps. You must never name, in writing or otherwise, the children who have lice. Exclusion from the setting is not required. Discourage the sharing of hairbrushes, hair accessories and hats in the setting. If there is a persistent problem, designate a special head treatment weekend and request all parents to treat their child for head lice that weekend (HPU 2006).

CARING FOR CHILDREN IN HOSPITAL

Many children will be admitted to hospital at some stage in their childhood. This may be for a relatively minor procedure (e.g. having grommets inserted) or because of an acute illness (e.g. appendicitis). Regardless of the cause, all children who enter hospital will need special care. Being hospitalised is a stressful experience for young children and they will need support throughout.

Preparing the child

In cases of planned procedures the child may know in advance that they are being admitted to hospital. In this case the ECCE worker may, with parents' permission, help to prepare the child for hospital.

Parents and workers can prepare the child for a planned admission to hospital by talking about hospital as a cheerful place where doctors and nurses help to make people better. The hospital should never be spoken about as a scary place or in a negative way.

Children make sense of the world through play and play can be a great way to help prepare children for hospital. The child should be encouraged to play Doctors and Nurses with adults or peers. Toy doctors' kits are readily available and make a great prop for this type of imaginative play. The toy kits also have the advantage of helping the child to become familiar with doctors' instruments such as stethoscopes. There are many books and stories that cover the subject of hospitalisation and parents should source and read some of these stories as preparation for the experience.

The most important way to prepare the child for the hospital visit is to talk to them about it. Parents should reassure the child that they will be there as much as possible, and that the child will be coming home. It is important to pass on to the child, in a way they can understand, any information gathered from the doctor about what the procedure will entail. Explain to the child about X-rays, injections and blood tests and always tell the truth about what each involves.

Arriving at hospital

When the child goes to hospital, the parents should bring a favourite toy or blanket (no matter how scruffy) and soother or bottle (if used). These will act as a comfort object for the child and a link to home. If the child uses special words for food, the potty or a favourite toy, these should be explained to the nurse to avoid any confusion. Going into hospital can be a frightening experience and it is important that parents are present as much as possible in order to reassure the child. It's important to cuddle and play with the child to give them reassurance and to help as much as possible with their everyday care, such as feeding and toileting.

PLAY FOR SICK CHILDREN

Play is very important for sick children and it can help them to:

- communicate how they are feeling
- be distracted from physical pain and worries or stress
- understand what is happening and gain information – play can be used to explain procedures to a child; for example giving a teddy bear a pretend injection to make them feel better can help the child understand about injections
- act out their fears through role play or using props such as dolls
- have a sense of normality – play can provide a link to home and 'real life'.

A sick child in hospital may not be able to engage in their normal play routine. They may have restricted movement because of drips, or they may not be allowed to leave the bed. In this case soothing activities that can be engaged in while sitting down or in bed will be useful.

- Books and story CDs can help distract children from the situation.
- A 'Treasure Box' – a box or basket full of activities and toys – has a great novelty value and can be carried between home and hospital.
- Puzzles and board games can be played with in bed.
- Playing with playdough is an absorbing and relaxing activity for young children.
- Drawing and some art and craft activities can be done sitting down or in bed.
- DVDs played on a laptop or portable DVD player can be a great distraction.
- For older children who feel well enough, school work may be an option!

CASE STUDY: A CHILD IN HOSPITAL

Jane is five years old and is in Junior Infants in the local primary school. Over the last month she has been complaining of pains in her stomach and feeling sick. One morning after waking up Jane experienced an excruciating pain in her side. Her mother took her to the doctor, who diagnosed a possible case of appendicitis. Jane was admitted to the local hospital and underwent an appendectomy. Jane felt really bad when she went to the hospital. Her tummy was really sore and made her cry. Jane had never been to hospital before and she thought it smelled funny. When she got to the children's ward she met a nice nurse who was really friendly and wore a bright uniform. Jane's mother explained that the nurses and doctors were going to help to make her feel better. She promised she would stay with Jane.

After the operation Jane woke up feeling very funny. She felt like crying, but her mother stayed with her and helped her to feel better. Jane's father came too and brought some of Jane's favourite toys from home as well as her special teddy. This made Jane feel much better. Jane's grandmother came to visit and brought her a book to read with her mother. The boy in the story was in hospital, just like Jane. Jane had to stay in hospital for a few days after her operation. She couldn't move much because she was sore and she was on a drip that the nurses called 'Freddy'. Jane's parents were able to stay with her the whole time and this made Jane feel a lot better. The ward had a playroom and when Jane felt better she went down there. She met lots of other children and got to paint pictures and play with toys.

Now it's time for Jane to go home. She still feels a bit sore sometimes but the nurse says this will stop soon and she is glad the pain in her tummy has gone.

Signpost for reflection

Write a reflective entry on a time a child became sick while you were on placement. What did you and other staff members do? Use Gibbs' reflective cycle (see Chapter Eight) as a guide when writing the entry.

chapter four

Personal Care Routines in ECCE

LEARNING OUTCOMES

After reading this chapter you will be able to:

- perform personal care routines for babies, including nappy changing, bathing, and topping and tailing
- support parents and children through the toilet training process
- describe children's physical care needs, including care for the skin, hair and teeth.

INTRODUCTION

One of the most vital skills you will need to learn in your Child Health and Well-being module is how to perform physical care routines for the children in your care. To be an effective ECCE worker it is essential that you master the skills of nappy changing, bathing a baby and other personal care routines. This chapter also prepares you for the Skills Demonstration, which is worth 60% of your overall grade for the module.

CHILDREN'S BASIC NEEDS

ECCE settings aim to meet children's basic needs. Maslow's hierarchy of human needs (Maslow 1954) can be useful in planning to meet these needs.

Self-actualisation

Self-esteem

Love and belonging

Safety and security

Basic needs

Figure 4.1 Maslow's hierarchy of human needs

Physiological needs

The bottom layer in Maslow's hierarchy is our physiological or basic needs. These are the needs that must be met in order to stay alive. Children's basic needs in an ECCE setting include those shown in Figure 4.2.

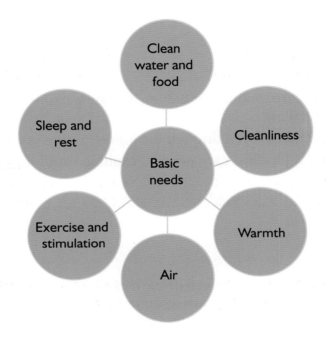

Figure 4.2 Children's basic needs

Children need clean water and food to stay alive. Their environment must be clean, hygienic and warm. They need plenty of fresh air and exercise. Children must be stimulated with toys and activities and they require quiet time for rest and sleep. If all these factors are present children's basic needs will be met.

Safety and security

Once our physiological needs are met, our need for safety and security becomes important. We need to be physically safe in our environment (Chapter Six discusses safety in an ECCE setting). We also need to feel emotionally safe, in other words to have relationships with others and attachment figures. (See Chapter Eight for a discussion of the importance of attachment.)

Love and belonging

Once our need for safety and security is met we need love and belonging. We need to feel loved and that we belong in social groups. The need for love and belonging can be met in an ECCE centre by operating a key worker system.

Self-esteem

Our need for self-esteem involves our need to feel good about ourselves. This can be met in the ECCE setting by praising children for their efforts, respecting children and displaying their work.

Self-actualisation

The final layer in Maslow's hierarchy is our need for self-actualisation. This refers to our need to fulfil our potential and 'be all we can be'. This need can be met by providing a varied and broad-based curriculum of activities for children.

> **THINK ABOUT IT**
>
> **How can we use Maslow's hierarchy of needs as a framework to plan for the provision of children's care in an ECCE setting?**

HOLDING A BABY

The first skill we are going to learn is how to pick up and hold a baby. You must hold the baby firmly but gently, making sure to support the head at all times. Figures 4.3 and 4.4 show how to pick up and hold a baby properly.

Picking up a newborn

- Slide one hand under the baby's neck to support the head, slide the other under the baby's back and bottom.
- Pick up the baby gently and smoothly.
- Hold the baby against your chest. This helps them feel safe and secure.
- Talk, chat and sing to the baby throughout to help the baby feel safe and secure.

Figure 4.3 Picking up a baby

Figure 4.4 Holding a baby against your chest makes them feel safe

Carrying an older baby

By the time a baby is four or five months old they can be carried in different ways.

» You can carry the baby on your hip – this allows them to look around and explore the world.
» You can hold the baby around the waist, facing forward so that they can look around.
» Many parents choose to use baby slings. These pieces of cloth allow the baby to be held against the parent. If using a baby sling it is important to make sure the nose, mouth and eyes are kept clear to avoid risk of suffocation.

NAPPIES

Nappy changing is a basic skill that all ECCE workers need to be fully competent in. Children will not be toilet trained until between 18 months and three years, depending on the child, so if you are based in a baby room, wobbler room or toddler room you will need to know how to change nappies. Some children with special educational needs may be late in developing control over their bladder and bowels, so staff in the pre-school room should also be competent at nappy changing.

There are two types of nappy: terry nappies, which are reusable; and disposable nappies, such as Pampers and Huggies. Parents will decide when their child is born which type to use for the child. Several factors will influence the parents' decision:

- The cost of each option. Terry nappies are more expensive in the short term, but the long-term cost of disposable nappies is greater as the terry nappies are reused.
- The time involved with each option. Terry nappies are more time-consuming because they have to be washed after each use.
- Hygiene factors. Some parents may consider disposable nappies more hygienic as the soiled nappies can be placed into a nappy sack and disposed of hygienically.
- Some parents may choose terry nappies due to environmental considerations – disposable nappies represent a serious environmental hazard. They can take up to 500 years to disintegrate and the average child can use up to 5,000 disposable nappies before being toilet trained! (Tipperary North County Council website.)

Disposable nappies are the most popular choice for parents of children in ECCE settings, so this chapter will focus on disposable nappies.

Disposable nappies are simple to use and dispose of. Parents will need a large supply of nappies – a newborn baby can use an average of ten nappies a day. There are many different brands and parents must choose the one that best suits the baby, based on absorbency, price and the shape and comfort of the nappy for the child. The baby's nappy must be changed every time they are soiled or wet, as well as first thing in the morning, last thing at night and after a bath.

Nappy changing equipment

- Unused disposable nappy.
- Nappy sack for the used nappy.
- Baby wipes.
- Sudocrem (if desired and in accordance with parents' wishes).
- Nappy changing mat.
- Disinfectant spray.
- Paper towels.

Procedure

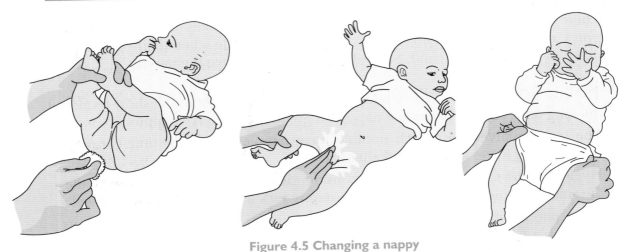

Figure 4.5 Changing a nappy

1 Gather all equipment needed.
2 Spray down the nappy changing mat with disinfectant spray.
3 Wash your hands and put on gloves and apron.
4 Pick up the baby, bring over to nappy changing area, lie the baby on nappy mat.
5 Undo bottom half clothes, undo the babygrow.
6 Open out the nappy and remove as much faeces as possible, scooping from back to front. Place discarded nappy in sack.
7 Lift the baby's legs using one hand and with the other use wet cotton wool to remove any remaining faeces. Use one piece of cotton wool per wipe and place used pieces in nappy sack.
8 Ensure you wipe from front to back, especially for baby girls – this prevents infection.
9 Dry area, apply barrier cream if desired.
10 Open out new nappy, lift baby's legs and slide nappy under baby.
11 Using both hands, bring the front of the nappy up between the legs. Close tabs.
12 Replace clothes, remove baby, wipe down mat, dispose of waste material.

Nappy changing is a great opportunity for some one-on-one bonding time with the baby. Talk, chat and sing to the baby throughout to make them feel safe and reassured.

Record keeping is very important in an ECCE setting. You will have to note what time you changed the baby's nappy, and if it was wet or dry, both in the nappy changing log and the child's daily record. A copy of this record must be made available to parents at the end of the day and another should be kept in the setting.

Table 4.1 Nappy changing: dos and don'ts

Do:	Don't:
Talk and sing to the baby as you change their nappy	Don't ever leave the baby unattended on the nappy changing mat for any reason
Gather all your equipment before you change the nappy	Don't ever wipe from back to front – this can cause infection
Remember to wash your hands before and after nappy changing and to wear gloves and an apron	Don't forget to make a note in the child's daily records and the nappy changing room's log of exactly when the nappy was changed and what type of nappy it was

Nappy rash

Nappy rash is the name given to occasional bouts of redness, blisters and soreness in the nappy area, i.e. the fold of skin in the groin area and around the genitals. Nappy rash is a common feature of babyhood and is very uncomfortable for the baby, so it should be minimised by taking precautionary measures.

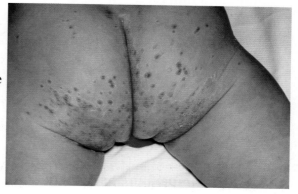

The root cause of nappy rash is the exposure of the bottom to urine and faeces for prolonged periods of time. The resulting dampness causes bacteria to develop, leading to the rash developing. For this reason children should **never** be left in a wet or dirty nappy. Poor nappy changing technique, which does not remove all the faeces from the nappy, can also be a cause. Bottle-fed babies' stools are more alkaline than those of breastfed babies, so breastfed babies are less likely to develop nappy rash (but this does not mean that they will never do so).

A second common cause of nappy rash is irritation of the nappy area from the friction of wearing a nappy. This can also be caused by a reaction to baby products. Babies who wear reusable nappies can develop nappy rash if the nappies are not rinsed properly. Nappy rash can also be caused by the yeast infection thrush.

Tips for preventing nappy rash

The best way to prevent nappy rash is by taking appropriate hygiene measures when nappy changing. Babies must never be left to sit in wet or soiled nappies. After bathing, the nappy area should be dried carefully to prevent dampness. Parents should try to expose the baby's bottom to the air for a few minutes as often as possible in order to allow the skin to breathe. Non-allergenic products should be used that will not irritate babies' sensitive skin. A barrier cream such as Sudocrem may prove useful for preventing nappy rash, but should not be overused as it will stop air from getting to the skin.

BATHING

The next core skill you must master is bathing. You may not have to bathe children in an ECCE setting as it is a task most parents will undertake at home. However, you must know how to bathe a baby: you may in the course of your career work as a nanny or au pair and in these jobs you might be expected to bathe children.

Young babies' skin is thin, and they get cold easily. For this reason the time spent undressed should be kept to a minimum and the bathing done in a warm room with a minimum temperature of 20°C.

Bathing equipment

- Baby bath.
- Baby bath lotion.
- Two towels.
- Cotton wool.
- Clean clothes.
- Bath toys/temperature gauge if desired.
- Clean nappy.
- Nappy changing mat.
- Baby wipes.

Procedure

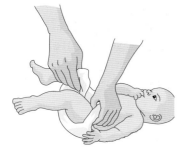

Figure 4.6 Bathing a baby

1   Gather all the equipment needed.

2   Wash your hands and put on a waterproof apron to protect your clothes.

3   Fill the bath 5–8cm deep; run the cold water tap first, then the hot. Check the temperature with your elbow – it should feel warm, **not** hot. If you have a temperature gauge, check that the temperature is 37°C.

4   Pick up the baby, undress the baby at the nappy changing mat, and wrap the baby in a dry towel. Clean the face and ears with moistened cotton wool.

5   Holding the baby under one arm, bring the baby to the bath. Lean over the bath, wash the baby's head and pat dry.

6   Bring the baby back to the nappy changing area. Remove the nappy and clean around the nappy area as normal. Wrap the baby in the towel.

7   Bring the baby to the bath and remove the towel. Lower the baby into the bath, feet first.

8   Support the baby by keeping one hand under the baby's head and shoulders. Wash with the other hand.

9   Lift the baby out of the bath into the towel. Dry thoroughly and dress.

Tips for bathing

Check the temperature of the water and make sure that it is not too hot. Remember, young babies have thinner skin than adults and will burn more easily. Temperature gauges designed as bath toys such as ducks are available and will give an accurate temperature reading. The water should be at 37°C. Very young babies cannot regulate their body temperature, so keep the time they are undressed to a minimum.

    Never, ever leave a baby or young child alone in a bath.

    Very young babies should be washed using water only, as soap will strip essential fatty acids from their skin.

Possible issues at bathtime

As any parent knows, bathtime can present some particular issues (see Figure 4.7).

Figure 4.7 Some possible problems at bathtime

Fear of undressing

Very small babies can become upset when they are undressed because they dislike the feeling of cold air on their skin. If the child becomes very distressed, do not force the issue: keep them clean by topping and tailing or with a sponge bath and try again at a later date.

Fear of bathing

Very small children may be afraid of bathing and the sensation of being wet. A baby who becomes very distressed at becoming wet should **never** be forced to bathe. Instead, help the child to become used to bathing by introducing them to water through play.

Fear of the big bath

Down the Drain, an episode of the TV programme *Rugrats,* describes how Tommy and Chucky develop a fear of the big bath. This can be a common experience for children. To try to overcome this, bathtime should be made into a fun experience for children. Bath toys can be used to help the child relax and enjoy the bathtime experience.

Dislike of hair washing

Dislike of hair washing is common in children under six. Young children may dislike the sensation of water on their head and the discomfort of shampoo in their eyes. Children should not be forced to have their hair washed if they are becoming genuinely upset. It can help to get the children to hold a facecloth over their eyes or use an eye shield. 'No tears' shampoos may also help.

TOPPING AND TAILING

Bathing is a time-consuming activity; topping and tailing is a quick and efficient alternative way to clean a baby. Topping and tailing means washing a baby's face, hands and nappy area, without undressing them completely.

Equipment

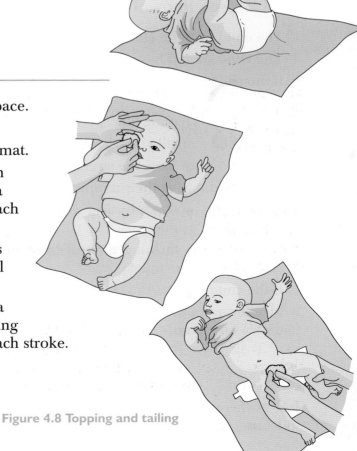

- Cotton wool balls.
- Bowl of lukewarm water.
- Clean nappy.
- Nappy changing mat and equipment.

Procedure

1 Gather equipment and prepare the space.
2 Wash your hands.
3 Pick up baby and place on changing mat.
4 Wet a cotton wool ball and wipe each eye from the inner corners out. Use a clean piece for each stroke and for each eye.
5 Wipe face, ears and neck, then hands and feet. Use a clean cotton wool ball each time.
6 Remove nappy and clean nappy area with moistened cotton wool balls, using a separate piece of cotton wool for each stroke. Change nappy as normal.

Figure 4.8 Topping and tailing

TOILET TRAINING

The art of toilet training is knowing when to encourage and knowing when to simply wait. (Coleman 2007:190)

Toilet training is an important developmental task for children. The psychologists Sigmund Freud and Erik Erikson both believed that toilet training is a key time for children's developing personality. ECCE workers are often involved in helping to toilet train the children in their care. As always, you must take your lead from the parents, although you can give advice and support.

There is a lot of debate on the best time to toilet train children. As with so many developmental tasks, there is no **right** time; each child will be different. Most children will be ready to for and achieve toilet training between 18 months and three years, but in general the earlier children start to be toilet trained the longer it takes.

Important note: You cannot force a child who is not ready to be toilet trained. The child must be ready to be trained. Parents must take their lead from the child.

How do you know if a child is ready to be toilet trained?

- The child must be able to walk to the toilet and sit down on the toilet.
- The child should have the words to describe stools and urine.
- If the child is having regular bowel movements at relatively predictable times, this can provide the opportunity to introduce the child to sitting on the potty.
- If the child is having 'dry' periods of at least three to four hours.
- If the child can tell you when they need to go or when they have gone to the toilet.
- The child must have the strength and dexterity to pull their pants up and down.
- If the child tugs at their nappy when wet or dirty.
- If the child makes physical actions when having a bowel movement – facial expressions, grunting.
- If the child is showing interest in others' bathroom habits – and they may be fascinated by the toilet.
- If the child dislikes the feeling of being in a dirty nappy.
- Most important, if the child isn't resistant to learning to use the toilet – if they are they won't learn!

How to toilet train

Just as there is **no right time** to be toilet trained, there is **no one correct way** to toilet train a child. However, the following tips may be useful.

- Before toilet training commences, introduce the child to the potty in play so they become familiar with it.
- You could role play using dolls and teddies to show the child how to use the potty.
- Books and popular children's TV shows often deal with toilet training. Source these materials and explore them with the child.
- Getting the child to help to pick out their underwear can be a reinforcing experience and help to make children interested in toilet training.
- Don't force the child to sit on the potty until they are comfortable. Initially, let them sit on the potty once a day fully clothed as routine.
- Allow the child to leave the potty at any time.
- Once the child is comfortable sitting on the potty fully clothed, let them sit there without a nappy/pants.
- Keep the child in pants that are easily pulled up and down.
- Training pants/pull-up pants can be used, but some parents choose not to do so as they think they can confuse the child. As with so much else it depends on the child.
- Praise the child for every attempt, whether successful or not.
- Accidents will happen during toilet training – never, ever reprimand the child for these.

EXERCISE

Do some research online to find resources you can get to support a child through toilet training. *Hint:* check books and DVDs of popular children's television shows.

Dealing with accidents

Accidents are part and parcel of toilet training. Toddlers can become distracted or absorbed in play and do not listen to their body's signals, resulting in accidents. How the adult reacts to the accident is very important. The adult must not criticise the child for the accident but should simply state in a matter-of-fact way what has happened. Children generally become dry by day first and may take some time to become dry at night.

BEDWETTING

Bedwetting is defined as involuntary urination during sleep that happens more often than once a month. It affects both boys and girls but is more common in boys. Bedwetting up to the age of five is not unusual as the child is still learning to control their bladder. One in 12 children aged between four and 12 years have wet the bed at some stage (*Irish Independent* 2010). If the child continues to bed wet past the age of five years, intervention may be necessary. It is not known what leads to bedwetting, but causes may include:

- slow maturation of the nervous system which controls the bladder
- a temporary underlying illness such as a urinary tract infection
- a small bladder which does not hold as much urine or an overactive bladder which gives the signal of fullness before full capacity is reached
- drinking before going to bed
- family history of bedwetting
- if the child is experiencing stressful life events, such as an illness or death in the family, they may begin to wet the bed despite previously being dry.

Helping a child who wets the bed

Parents may ask you for advice on how to cope with a child who wets the bed. You should be able to offer some tips and advice on how to deal with the situation in a positive manner.

- Protect the bed mattress with a plastic cover.
- Make sure the child goes to the toilet before going to bed.
- Respond gently and patiently to accidents – don't blame, criticise or punish the child.
- Give rewards for staying dry – a star chart may be useful for showing the child's progress.
- Give the children less to drink late in the evenings so their bladder is empty when they go to bed.
- Some parents find it useful to wake the child to go to the toilet after they have been asleep for a few hours; however, this may not work in the long term.

CARE FOR CHILDREN'S SKIN AND HAIR

Skin

Young babies do not need to be washed often, but as children grow and become more active a daily bath or shower becomes necessary. In addition, children should be taught to wash their face and hands every morning and their hands after going to the toilet. Children's nails should be kept clean and short, cut straight across. Adults should ensure that skin is thoroughly dried after washing: this is particularly important for black skin, which tends to dryness and may need a special moisturiser.

The navel

The navel is clamped after delivery, leaving a two- to three-inch stump. This shrivels and falls off within a few days. The wound will have to be given time to heal and should be exposed to air as much as possible to promote this.

Hair

Cradle cap

In the first year of life children can experience cradle cap, a thick scaly rash that appears on the scalp. It is harmless and the cause is unknown. Regular washing of the hair and soft brushing of the scalp may help to treat cradle cap, as will massaging oils into the scalp.

Older children's hair need only be washed twice a week. A conditioning shampoo may be used for children with long or curly hair to prevent tangles. Wet hair should be combed, not brushed, as brushing breaks the hair shaft. Children of African descent may have dry hair, which will need special oil or moisturiser.

CARE FOR CHILDREN'S FEET

Young children's feet are soft and supple because the bones are not yet rigid. As the feet grow they change shape. Because of this, care must be taken with young children's feet as they can easily be damaged.

Foot care guidelines

- Wash and dry feet every day.
- Cut toenails straight across and keep them short.
- Allow the child to go barefoot as much as possible.
- Do not buy proper leather shoes until the child is walking properly. Wearing leather shoes too early can restrict the child's growth.

▶ Children's shoes should be properly fitted by a trained professional and should be of good-quality material.

▶ Children's feet should be measured regularly to make sure shoes fit properly, with room for growth.

▶ There should always be a one-centimetre gap between the longest toe and the inside of the shoe.

Foot problems

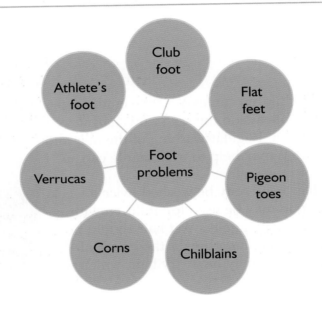

Figure 4.9 Foot problems that can occur in childhood

Club foot

Club foot is a condition in which the baby is born with one or both feet twisted out of shape. It can be caused by the foot staying in a fixed position in the womb. It can be treated with exercises, strapping or, in extreme cases, surgery.

Flat feet

Flat feet are caused by ligaments and muscles not developing properly. It is relatively rare in children.

Pigeon toes

This is when the toes point outwards as the legs/feet are rotated. It is common in children and usually corrects itself by the age of seven.

Chilblains

Chilblains are red, itchy swollen areas on the feet that are caused by the narrowing of blood vessels in cold weather. They usually heal without treatment but are uncomfortable. Chilblains can be prevented by wrapping up warm in cold weather.

Corns

Corns are thickened areas of skin on the toes. They are usually caused by ill-fitting shoes. Corns can be pared down by a doctor or chiropodist.

Verrucas

A verruca is a small growth caused by the human papilloma virus. Verrucas are passed on by contact with an infected person or recently shed skin flakes and they develop in warm, moist conditions. Flat verrucas, which occur on the soles of the feet, are often spread by walking barefoot in swimming pool changing areas. They can be treated with cream or removed by a GP by freezing, scraping or burning.

Athlete's foot

Athlete's foot, which is relatively rare in children, is a fungal skin condition producing cracked, sore and itchy skin between the toes. It is spread by walking barefoot in communal areas such as changing rooms. It can be treated by anti-fungal treatments and can be prevented by encouraging good hygiene measures such as washing feet and changing socks daily.

CHOOSING CLOTHING FOR CHILDREN

When choosing clothes for children the following criteria should be followed.

- **Hardwearing:** Are the clothes made of material that will withstand the rough and tumble of play, especially outdoor play?
- **Comfortable:** Children do not like wearing uncomfortable clothes; clothes should be easy to move in and to wear.
- **Washable:** Children's clothes should be easily washable.
- **Easy to pull on and off:** Young children are developing the dexterity to dress themselves; clothing that is easy to pull on and off will help them do this.

In general, children will need the following items of clothing:

- underwear
- sleepwear
- day clothes
- outdoor gear
- clothes for wet weather, e.g. raincoat and wellies
- 'good' clothes for special occasions such as family celebrations – these are usually bought specially for the occasion.

Children will get dirty in day-to-day play – it is part of childhood! Adults should not criticise a child for getting their clothes dirty during normal play.

THINK ABOUT IT

What kind of clothes should children be dressed in for pre-school?

DENTAL CARE FOR 0–6-YEAR-OLDS

Dental care begins at birth, and good dental care from an early age will give children the best start in life for oral health. There are three types of teeth: incisors, canines and molars. Incisors are the centre four flat teeth, which are used for biting food. Canine teeth are positioned beside the incisors and are sharp, pointed teeth used for tearing food. Molars are the big back teeth used to grind food.

Teething

Every child is born with a complete set of teeth under the gums. Babies can start teething from 13 weeks, although this will vary from child to child. By the time the child is six or seven months the first teeth will have appeared and the child will have 20 teeth by the age of two or two and a half years. These early teeth are called milk teeth and will be replaced by 32 adult permanent teeth in middle childhood. The first two teeth to come through come on the bottom gum, followed in one or two months by the two top teeth. This pattern repeats until all 20 teeth are present.

Baby teeth are important for the following reasons:

- They help the child to bite and chew food.
- They act as a guide for the adult teeth to grow and develop.
- They enable speech and the formation of certain sounds.
- Healthy baby teeth are important for the child's self-confidence.

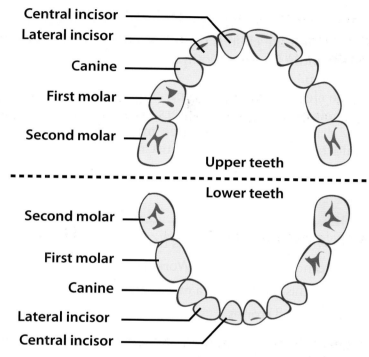

Figure 4.10 Milk teeth

Signs that children are teething

- Flushed cheeks.
- Dribbling, which may cause chafing and irritation around the neck.
- Chewing the fist or toys more than usual.
- Sore, tender gums around the site of the new tooth.
- The child may be off their food and sleeping poorly at night.
- Nappy rash.

How to help a teething child

- Give the child something to chew on, e.g. a cool teething ring or rusk.
- Massage gums with sugar-free teething gels or a finger.

▶ Parents may choose to give mild sugar-free pain relief medication at night if the child wakes and is irritable.

▶ Cold winds can make teething worse, so the child should be wrapped up well with a hat and scarf when taken outside.

Caring for teeth

Once teeth appear they should be cleaned with a soft wash cloth daily. Toothpaste should not be used until the child is two years old, and then they can use a pea-sized amount of child-friendly fluoride toothpaste. Parents must supervise tooth brushing until the chid is seven.

Teeth should be cleaned every morning and evening. Never leave the child asleep with a bottle in their mouth or dip soothers into sugar, syrup or honey. Avoid giving the child sugary drinks and use sugar-free medication to protect teeth from decay. The child should be brought to the dentist regularly, starting at around their first birthday.

EXERCISE

As part of your setting's curriculum it has been decided to hold a 'Keep your teeth clean' week to promote oral hygiene. Working in small groups, devise a plan for the week to reflect this theme. Use a mix of activities, songs, guests invited to the setting, art and craft, and stories.

Signpost for reflection

Think of a time you performed a personal care routine for a child on placement. Use Gibbs' reflective cycle (see Chapter 8) to describe the experience and how you can improve in future.

Section Two

NUTRITION, HEALTH AND SAFETY

Nutrition in the ECCE Setting

After reading this chapter you will be able to:

▶ evaluate the advantages and disadvantages of breastfeeding and bottle-feeding
▶ outline the steps involved in weaning a baby on to solids
▶ discuss the food pyramid and various nutrients
▶ plan nutritious, well-balanced meals for the children in your care
▶ accommodate any special dietary requirements children may have.

INTRODUCTION

All children need the right nutrition to grow healthy and strong. This chapter will teach you about healthy eating for children from birth until school age. Babies and toddlers grow at such a rapid rate that it is really important that parents and ECCE workers spend time planning how to meet children's nutritional needs.

FEEDING YOUNG BABIES: BREAST OR BOTTLE?

One of the first decisions new parents must make is whether to breastfeed or bottle-feed their newborn. When formula milk was first introduced, breastfeeding went somewhat out of fashion, and between 1981 and 1991 the rate of breastfeeding in Ireland was 32% (DoHC 2005). However, over the last twenty years public health campaigns have encouraged a higher rate of breastfeeding. Fifty per cent of Irish mothers now breastfeed (Williams & Greene 2010), and more educated mothers are most likely to breastfeed their children. Irish mothers still do not breastfeed as much as mothers in the rest of Europe, and most of those who do stop breastfeeding within the first three months, far earlier than the WHO's recommendation of two years.

Breast milk is the baby's natural and preferred food choice. Human milk is tailor-made for babies' nutritional needs and contains just the right amount of protein, carbohydrates, minerals and vitamins to sustain the growing baby. It is thus recommended that all new mothers breastfeed, if only for a short period of time. The first milk the mother produces is called **colostrum**, a yellow liquid high in beta carotene, protein and antibodies.

Many children will be on bottle feed only by the time they enter an ECCE setting, so this chapter will teach you how to make up a bottle feed as well as how to promote breastfeeding.

Storage of breast milk

Many mothers choose to express breast milk into a bottle by using a breast pump. This is useful as it means that an adult other than the mother can feed the child and that breastfeeding can continue when the mother returns to work. Expressed breast milk can be stored at room temperature for up to six hours or in a fridge for up to five days. It can also be frozen and stored for up to three months. If breast milk has been frozen it should be thawed slowly in the fridge. A microwave should **never** be used to thaw frozen breast milk as this can lead to 'hot spots' forming in the milk.

Advantages of breastfeeding

▶ Breast milk is convenient and time-efficient; there is no need to make up formula or to sterilise feeding equipment (unless the mother is expressing milk into bottles). This makes breastfeeding a far more efficient feeding choice.
▶ It is produced at body temperature, so it is always the right temperature for feeding.
▶ It is digested more quickly and easily than cow's milk or formula milk.
▶ Babies who are breastfed pass fewer stools, don't get constipated and are less prone to nappy rash.

Long-term health benefits of breastfeeding

Recent research investigating the potential long-term health benefits of breastfeeding indicates that breastfed babies are less likely than bottle-fed babies to be overweight as children. Some evidence suggest benefits of breastfeeding in intellectual development and perceptual development – children who are breastfed score higher on measures of both. In general, breastfed babies are less prone to illness because breast milk contains antibodies against disease which are carried from the mother, and this will boost the child's natural immunity.

Research has also found that long-term benefits of breastfeeding include:

▶ lower risk of respiratory illness in later childhood
▶ lower probability of developing allergies in childhood
▶ lower blood pressure in childhood
▶ lower risk of developing diabetes
▶ lower cholesterol in childhood
▶ lower risk of ear infections
▶ lower incidence of coeliac disease.

(www.breastfeeding.ie)

THINK ABOUT IT

Breastfeeding levels in Ireland are still below the European average. How could we promote breastfeeding and encourage more mothers to breastfeed?

Disadvantages of breastfeeding

▶ Unless the mother chooses to express the milk, all the feeding must be done by her. This can place an extra workload on her.
▶ While the mother is breastfeeding the baby eats whatever she eats, so she must continue to watch her diet – no alcohol, painkillers, etc.
▶ The father and other relations/friends do not have the chance to bond with the child through bottle-feeding unless the mother expresses the milk using a breast pump.
▶ A small minority of mothers do not produce enough milk for the baby or may develop sore breasts and find it difficult to breastfeed.

For these reasons or because of personal choice the parents may decide to bottle-feed their child with formula milk. There are many different brands available on the market and it may take parents some time to decide which brand best suits their child's needs. Formula milk is designed to meet the child's nutritional requirements.

Bottle-feeding

Making a formula feed

1 Boil fresh tap water in a kettle or covered saucepan.
2 When the water has boiled, leave it to cool for 30 minutes, but no longer. This will kill any bacteria.

3 Clean the work surface with disinfectant spray, and wash your hands with soap and water.

4 Read the instructions on the label to see how much powder to water is needed. A general rule of thumb is one scoop per fluid ounce (30ml).

5 Pour the right amount of boiled water into a sterile bottle, measuring the level at the lowest point of the water.

6 Add the exact amount of formula, using the scoop provided. Make sure there are no lumps in the mixture and that you only add the exact amount required.

7 Screw the bottle lid on tightly and shake well to mix the contents.

8 Test the temperature of the mix on the inside of your wrist. If it's too hot, hold the bottle under cold running water.

 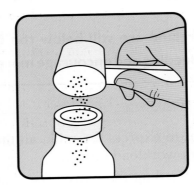 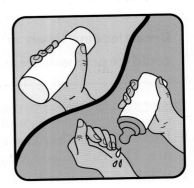

Figure 5.1 Preparing a formula feed

Feeding

1 Having prepared the feed, sit down with the child in your arms. You will need a towel for winding the child.

2 Stimulate the rooting reflex by placing the teat in the corner of the child's mouth. The child will then open their mouth and you can place the teat of the bottle fully in the mouth.

3 Tilt the bottle so that the hole in the teat is always covered with milk.

4 Talk to the baby throughout as you give the feed.

5 Wind the baby as necessary.

Tips

▶ Prepare bottle feed as required to prevent bacteria growth.

▶ Any unused feed should be thrown away after 24 hours.

▶ When making the feed, be careful not to compress the powder or to use lumpy powder, as this can lead to the feed becoming over-concentrated.

▶ Make sure the scoop is filled to the top and that there are no air pockets to ensure that you are preparing the correct amount of formula.

Storage of formula feed

Parents may choose to make up bottles of formula milk in batches instead of making a fresh feed on demand. Pre-made bottles of formula can be stored in a fridge for 24 hours. Leftover feed should be discarded after two hours. When heating a bottle, sit the bottle in a jug of warm water for 15 minutes. **Never** use a microwave to re-heat feeds: microwaves heat unevenly and this can cause hot spots, which can scald the baby's mouth.

Packets of pre-made formula feed are also available and are useful when going on journeys with children. Parents whose children are still using bottles should bring a supply of pre-made formula in a cool bag to the setting each day. The bottles must then be placed in the fridge and labelled so that the right feed goes to the right child.

FEEDING ABNORMALITIES IN BABIES

During a baby's first year some problems with feeding, such as wind, colic and reflux, may arise.

Wind

Wind occurs when the baby swallows air while feeding, usually when feeding too fast or too slowly. The trapped air causes the baby to feel uncomfortable or full and to cry, squirm or stop feeding.

Wind is a normal part of feeding and is easily treated by 'winding' the baby. At the end of the feed, place the baby over your shoulder or across your lap and pat or rub their back gently to help the baby to burp and relieve the trapped wind. You may need to put a towel on your shoulder to protect your clothes as sometimes the baby brings up small amounts of milk while being winded. This is called posseting.

Colic

Babies with colic have spells of non-stop inconsolable crying and irritability. Colic affects both breastfed and bottle-fed babies. It is not known exactly what causes colic, but it is thought to be related to a build-up of wind, overstimulation or gut contractions caused by lactose intolerance. Most babies outgrow colic between four and six months. Parents can take steps to reduce colic by rocking the baby, baby massage, reducing wind by using special bottles and not changing breasts too quickly when breastfeeding. Some over-the-counter remedies are also available at chemists.

Reflux

Reflux occurs when small quantities of milk are vomited up soon after feeding. Reflux affects 50% of babies. Most babies grow out of reflux and it is usually not serious if the baby is gaining weight and otherwise well. Reflux can be managed by reducing the volume of feeds, avoiding moving the baby straight after a feed and winding the baby. However, if the reflux is persistent or excessive, further measures may be needed. The GP or public health nurse will advise parents on options, which may include using a thickened formula or using Gaviscon Infant formula.

If a child in your care shows signs of reflux, record the time and a description of the reflux and notify the parents at the end of the day.

WEANING ON TO SOLIDS

'Weaning' is the term given to the gradual introduction of solid foods into the diet. For the first few months of a baby's life, breast/bottle milk provides all the nutrients needed. However, as the baby grows they will need a more varied diet. This usually happens between four and six months. Bottle-fed babies will need to be weaned earlier than breastfed babies. It is important not to wean babies any earlier than four months as their digestive system is still maturing and is not able to process solid foods. Babies should not be weaned any later than six months: if weaning is left any later children may be reluctant to start eating solids.

Beginning to wean

Before weaning can begin you will need a baby bowl and spoon, steriliser and liquidiser or blender. New foods should be introduced one at a time, starting with small amounts (one tablespoon) and gradually building up to larger amounts.

The first foods should be smooth, with no lumps. Breast milk/formula milk or cooled boiled water can be added to get the purée to the right consistency. You can make your own food or purchase processed baby food, but if you make your own you can control for salt, sugar and additives. Homemade food will also taste better and be more varied for the baby.

It is best to start weaning in the afternoon, when the baby is most alert. There are three stages in weaning, as shown in Table 5.1.

Table 5.1 Stages in weaning

Stage	Food	Consistency	Drink	Foods not to be given
Stage 1	▶ Puréed meat, peas and beans ▶ Puréed fruit/vegetables ▶ Puréed potatoes ▶ Gluten-free cereal	Food should be puréed and of a soft consistency with no lumps	▶ Breast milk or bottle feed ▶ Cooled boiled water	▶ Any foods containing gluten ▶ Nuts ▶ Eggs ▶ Cow's milk
Stage 2	▶ Well-cooked eggs ▶ Cereals ▶ Bread, pasta ▶ Cheese	Minced, mashed or finely chopped	▶ Breast or formula milk ▶ Cooled boiled water ▶ Very dilute juice (1 part juice to 4–5 parts water)	▶ Nuts ▶ Unpasteurised cheese ▶ Eggs
Stage 3 (9–12 months)	A variety of foods can be given	Chopped and mashed	As for Stage 2	As for Stage 2

Source: HPU 2006

Finger foods

As children's fine motor skills develop they should be encouraged to self-feed using finger foods – foods that are easily picked up in the pincer grasp. This can take place when the baby is aged between seven and nine months.

Examples of finger food include:

▶ cheese slices or cubes
▶ ripe peeled fruit

‣ cooked soft vegetables
‣ buttered toast (without the crust).

Self-feeding should be encouraged as much as possible. It can be messy, but it is a vital social skill the child must master. Once weaning has been completed the child will need to take in adequate food for their day-to-day requirements.

Foods to avoid giving babies

‣ **Salt** is toxic to babies because their kidneys cannot process it properly. It should *never* be added to babies' food.
‣ Foods containing **gluten** should not be given to children under one year as it can cause gluten intolerance later in life.
‣ **Nuts** should not be given to children under five years as they are a choking hazard.
‣ **Whole eggs** should not be given to babies under eight months.
‣ Do not give **spinach**, **turnip** or **beetroot** to a baby under six months.
‣ **Cow's milk** should be avoided until the baby is a year old, but it can be used to soften food.

> **Iron**
> Babies are born with a store of iron, but this is depleted during the first six months of life as both breast milk and formula milk are poor sources of iron. When babies start to be weaned, iron-rich foods such as green leafy vegetables and lean meat should be included to boost their stores of iron.

FOOD REFUSAL

Food refusal is a repeated refusal to eat, chew or swallow food. Food refusal can be common in toddlers, who may be too busy having fun and exploring the world to eat! Food refusal is also one of the ways toddlers express their independence and personality – remember, it is during the toddler years that the child starts to say 'No!'

Food refusal can also be as a result of the child engaging in bad feeding habits that affect their appetite. These can include:

‣ Drinking too much juice/soft drinks/diluted drinks. If toddlers consume more than two glasses of these drinks a day it will fill up their stomach and thus reduce their appetite.
‣ Drinking too much cow's milk or formula milk will also affect a child's appetite.

▶ A child who is given too many treat foods or who is 'grazing' and snacking continually throughout the day may not be hungry at mealtimes.

Many children will occasionally have 'off days' when they do not eat well. However, if the child has been eating poorly for a number of days and is not unwell it may be a case of food refusal. Several steps can be taken to deal with food refusal.

▶ Make a list of everything the child is eating and drinking during the day. If the child is drinking a lot of fluids or eating a lot of treat foods, decrease the amount of these that are offered to the child.

▶ Check when the child is eating. It may be that the child is grazing during the day and is simply not hungry at mealtimes. If this is the case, stop the grazing and standardise mealtimes. Mealtimes should be regular and familiar: children thrive on routine!

▶ Make mealtimes a family occasion free of distractions. Children learn by watching others, especially their parents and siblings. If the family eats together the child will be more likely to want to eat with their family.

▶ Never bribe or force a child to eat.

THE FOOD PYRAMID

The food pyramid is a visual guide to a healthy diet and is designed to illustrate how to plan for a balanced diet. The most recent version of the food pyramid was launched by the Department of Health and Children in June 2012.

Each type of food is represented by a shelf on the pyramid with a recommendation for the number of portions per day. (A portion might be one slice of wholemeal bread or one medium-sized apple.) There is an adapted version of the food pyramid for children that shows child-appropriate portion sizes.

Group one: breads and cereals

Breads and cereals (and pasta, rice, etc.), which provide most of our energy requirements, should make up most of our diet. Children aged one to three need four servings of breads and cereals a day, and four- to six-year-olds need four to six servings of bread and cereals a day. Adults need six or more servings of bread and cereals daily, depending on activity level.

Understanding the Food Pyramid

Top Shelf foods are high in fat, sugar and salt, are not essential for health and taken in excess can be harmful.

Fats and oils are essential, but only in small amounts.

The foods and drinks on the bottom 4 shelves of the Food Pyramid are essential for good health.

Maximum   1

Choose any   2

Choose any   2

Choose any   3

Choose any   5+

Choose any   6+

From http://www.safefood.eu/Healthy-Eating/Food-Diet/What-is-a-balanced-diet/The-Food-Pyramid.aspx

Group two: fruit and vegetables

This group includes all types of fruit and vegetable. This group is really important for providing the body with essential vitamins and minerals and is also a source of fibre. Our recommended intake of this group increases with age.

Table 5.2 Daily fruit and vegetable requirements

Age	Fruit and vegetable requirements
1–3	2–4 portions daily
4–5	4–5 portions daily
5+	4–6 portions daily
Adults	5 portions daily

Group three: milk and dairy products

Group three is made up of milk, cheese and yoghurt. Dairy products are very important for young children as they are high in calcium, which is needed for healthy bones. Children need three portions of milk and dairy products daily, but for children between nine and 18 this increases to five portions daily. An adult needs three portions of dairy products daily.

Group four: meat and pulses

This group includes meat, fish and non-meat sources of protein such as eggs and pulses (beans and peas). This group provides us with our protein intake and is needed for healthy growth. Children and adults should eat two portions of meat and/or pulses daily.

Group five: fats and oils

Group five is made up of fats and oils used in cooking and food preparation. Foods in this group include butter, margarine and vegetable oil. Children and adults should limit their intake of this group to two servings daily.

Group six: foods high in fats, salt and sugar

Group six is what is commonly known as 'junk food', for example biscuits, chocolate, sweets and crisps. Intake of this group needs to be restricted to a maximum of one serving a day. Four squares of chocolate is equivalent to one serving.

NUTRIENTS FOR HEALTH

The food pyramid is designed to show the amount of nutrients a person needs every day. A nutrient is a chemical needed by the body for growth and day-to-day functioning. Humans need three main nutrients in their daily diet: carbohydrates; lipids (fats); and protein. We also need a range of vitamins and minerals.

Carbohydrates

Carbohydrates are needed by the body to provide energy and heat. Carbohydrates are the body's preferred energy source and are most easily converted into energy. Excess carbohydrates are turned into fat, which insulates the body and helps keep the person warm. There are three types of carbohydrates: starch; fibre; and sugar.

Starch

Starch is needed to provide energy. In digestion, starchy carbohydrates are broken down and converted to glucose, which is the body's preferred energy source. Sources of starch include pasta, flour, bread and cereals.

Fibre

Also known as roughage, fibre cannot be broken down by the body but is used to get rid of undigested foodstuffs from the bowel, keeping the bowel and gut healthy. Inadequate fibre in the diet can cause constipation. Fruit, vegetables, wholemeal bread, brown rice and brown pasta are all good sources of fibre.

Sugar

Sugar is quickly converted into energy. There are four types of sugar: lactose, which is found in milk; glucose, found in breads and cereals; fructose, found in fruit; and sucrose, which is the refined sugar we add to food. Sucrose is not essential in the diet and its intake should be limited. Children who eat a lot of sugar and foods that are high in sugar are at risk of conditioning their taste buds to prefer sugary food. Many processed foods are also high in sugar because it is used as a preservative, to make the food taste better, and to disguise and bulk out poor-quality food.

Effects of sugar:

▶ mood swings
▶ tooth decay
▶ weight gain
▶ increased risk of type II diabetes.

> **Warning!**
> 'No added sugar' does not mean that the food is low in sugar, just that no sugar has been added. The foodstuff may still be high in natural sugars. For example, some juices are marketed as 'no added sugar', but this does not mean that they are low in sugar!

Lipids (fats)

Fats or lipids are important in the diet to provide energy, essential fatty acids and fat-soluble vitamins. Fat makes food taste good and is needed to insulate the body and protect the internal organs from damage.

There are two types of fat: saturated and unsaturated. Both are needed by the body in different amounts. Saturated fats are found in animal sources such as butter, eggs, cheese, meat, fish and lard and are solid at room temperature. Unsaturated fats are 'healthy' fats and are liquid at room temperature. They come from vegetable and plant sources such as nuts, cereals and vegetable oil. There are two sub-types of unsaturated fats; polyunsaturated fats and monounsaturated fats.

Polyunsaturated fats are also known as essential fatty acids, omega-3 and omega-6. These are needed for healthy brain development and to lower cholesterol.

Omega-3 and omega-6 are found in nuts, oily fish and fish oils, and current research suggests that they may have a role to play in increasing attention and concentration in children with attention deficit hyperactivity disorder (ADHD) and autism.

Monounsaturated fats are found in olives, olive oil and peanuts and are needed for a healthy heart and to reduce 'bad' cholesterol in the bloodstream.

> **Trans fat**
> Trans fat (usually labelled as hydrogenated fat) is a type of saturated fat found in processed foods that has been found to substantially increase cholesterol. It is recommended that we limit our intake of trans fats to as close to zero as possible.

Protein

Protein is an essential nutrient for healthy growth and development. Protein is made up of amino acids, which are the building blocks for our cells. Protein is essential for the growth and repair of the body's cells and is vital for the growing child.

There are two types of protein: first- and second-class protein. First-class protein, which comes from animal sources (meat, fish and eggs) and from soya, provides all the amino acids we need. Second-class protein comes from vegetable sources including nuts, pulses, bread and pasta. These foods contain only some of the amino acids needed by the body.

Protein is also a source of heat and energy and contains hormones and enzymes needed for a healthy body. Protein deficiency can lead to delayed growth, poor healing of wounds, lack of energy and increased susceptibility to illness.

Vitamins

A vitamin is an organic compound required by our body as a nutrient. Vitamins can be fat- soluble (A, D, E and K) or water-soluble (B and C). This section will describe the sources and uses of the most important vitamins in our diet.

Vitamin A

Vitamin A is needed for healthy growth, skin, eyes and bones and to fight infections, in particular nose and throat infections. It is found in dairy products and eggs. For maximum absorption, Vitamin A should be taken with beta-carotene, found in carrots, red peppers and sweetcorn. If children lack vitamin A, it restricts their growth and can cause night blindness: 500,000 children in the poorest counties of the world go blind every year from vitamin A deficiency. Children aged one to five need 400µg of vitamin A every day. Although a deficiency of vitamin A is dangerous, too much vitamin A is also dangerous and it can be poisonous in large amounts.

Vitamin B

The B group of vitamins is found in nuts, pulses, vegetables, cereals, brown bread, fish, milk, cheese and eggs. There are 13 different B vitamins, the most important being vitamins B1, B2, B6, B9 and B12.

▶ **Vitamin B1**, also known as thiamine, is found in wholegrain cereals, fortified cereals, pork, meat, eggs and milk. It is needed for the healthy development of the nervous system and the release of energy from carbohydrates. Deficiencies in thiamine can lead to delayed growth in children.

▶ **Vitamin B2** (riboflavin) is found in meat, milk, eggs, cheese and green vegetables. It is needed for growth in children, healthy skin and the formation of red blood cells. Vitamin B2 deficiency can cause a swollen red tongue, increased infections and delayed growth.

▶ **Vitamin B6** is made up of two substances, niacin and pyridoxine. Niacin is found in meat, bread, potatoes and fortified cereals and is needed for the release of energy from carbohydrates. Pyridoxine is found in meat, fish and poultry, green leafy vegetables, bananas and melon. It is needed for the release of energy and the formation of red and white blood cells. It also plays a role in the transmission of nerve impulses around the body.

▶ **Vitamin B9/folic acid** is found in green leafy vegetables and helps form red blood cells. Folic acid has a major role in preventing neural tube defects, including spina bifida, which has a high rate of occurrence in Ireland. Taking folic acid in pregnancy has been found to reduce the chances of the unborn baby developing spina bifida. Women planning on getting pregnant are advised to take folic acid for three months before and three months after conception.

▶ **Vitamin B12**, or cyancobalamin, is found in meat, salmon, cod, cheese and milk. It is needed for a healthy nervous system, the release of folic acid and production of red blood cells.

Vitamin C

Vitamin C is found in fruit and vegetables. The best sources of vitamin C include kiwi fruits and blackcurrants, citrus fruits such as oranges and lemons, and green vegetables. Vitamin C is essential for a healthy immune system, healthy growth and healthy skin and gums. Vitamin C assists in the absorption of non-meat sources of iron. It is water-soluble and cannot be stored in the body, which means that our diet must contain regular, adequate levels of vitamin C. If we do not take in enough vitamin C we become prone to illness. In extreme cases a deficiency of vitamin C can lead to scurvy, which causes weakness, bleeding gums and painful joints.

Vitamin D

Vitamin D is made by the skin when exposed to sun. It is also found in milk, eggs, cheese, cereals, liver, tuna, salmon and cod liver oil. It is needed by the body to absorb calcium and so contributes to healthy teeth and bones. Vitamin D also helps to regulate the amount of calcium stored by our body. Deficiencies in Vitamin D can lead to dental decay and in extreme cases **rickets**, which is the softening of bones in childhood leading to deformities such as bowed legs. Vitamin D can be poisonous in large amounts.

Vitamin E

Found in vegetable oils, brown bread, nuts, green leafy vegetables and egg yolk, vitamin E is used to protect body tissues, promote normal growth and help the body form red blood cells. Vitamin E also has a role in the absorption of vitamin A and is an anti-oxidant; it is thought to have a role in anti-ageing and the prevention of cancer. Vitamin E is found in most foods, so deficiency is rare. However, premature babies are often born with low stores of the vitamin and they will be put on special supplements by the neo-natal team to make up for the deficiency.

Vitamin K

Vitamin K is necessary for clotting the blood, so it has a significant role in wound healing. Vitamin K is also needed for the development of strong bones. Sources of vitamin K include green leafy vegetables, liver, cereals, fish and milk.

Minerals

Minerals are chemicals that occur naturally in food and that are required by the body. This section will explore the use of the minerals iron, calcium, phosphorus, potassium and sodium.

Iron

Iron is found in red meat and green leafy vegetables. It forms haemoglobin in the blood, which is needed to carry oxygen around the body. Mild iron deficiency leads to lack of energy and tiredness. Severe iron deficiency is known as **iron deficiency anaemia**, which causes the person to become pale, irritable, easily breathless and fatigued. Iron deficiency is a common problem, especially in women of child-bearing age. It is thought to be caused by several factors, including a poor diet that is low in iron, loss of blood from ulcers or menstruation or a poorly regulated vegetarian diet. It may also be due to a problem in **absorption** of iron, which can be improved by increasing vitamin C in the diet. Tea and coffee contain tannin, which interferes with iron absorption. It is estimated that 48% of Irish women aged 18–50 and 10% of Irish toddlers are iron deficient.

Babies are born with high reserves of iron, but these are depleted by the age of six months. Babies and toddlers need to take in iron, but milk is a poor source of iron. For this reason a baby's or toddler's diet should contain iron-rich food.

Table 5.3 Iron-rich foods for toddlers

Food	Portion	Iron content (mg)	% toddler's RDA
Beef	Two lean slices	2.9	29
Lamb	Two lean slices	2.4	24
Pork	Lean pork chop	1.1	11
Rashers	Two back rashers, grilled	0.9	9
Black pudding	Three slices	15	150
Liver	Two slices, fried	10	100
Chicken	Grilled chicken breast	0.5	5
Cod	Cod fillet	0.6	6
Wholemeal bread	Two slices	1.5	15
Egg	One boiled egg	1.2	12

To increase iron intake:

- Eat more meat. Meat contains haem iron, which is easily absorbed by the body.
- Non-haem iron is found in fortified foods and dark green vegetables, but non-haem iron is **not** easily absorbed by the body and should not be the only source of iron in the diet.
- Absorption of non-haem sources of iron can be boosted by taking Vitamin C with these sources.
- Avoid tea or coffee with meals as this interferes with iron absorption.

Calcium

Found in milk, milk products such as yoghurt and cheese, eggs and green vegetables, calcium is essential for the body to maintain and repair bones and teeth. Children aged one to ten need 800g of calcium per day, equivalent to four 200ml glasses of milk. Calcium is only absorbed by the body if taken with vitamin D. Deficiency in calcium can cause rickets and osteoporosis (brittle bones).

Phosphorus

Phosphorus is essential for life and is present in every cell in the body. It has functions in bone, teeth and cell production. Most foods contain phosphorus, but meat, fish, eggs, dairy, nuts and seeds are particularly good sources.

Potassium

Potassium is needed to generate nerve impulses, to regulate fluid intake and for muscle contraction, and it is also thought to have a role in regulating blood pressure. It is found in all four main food groups, but in particular in bananas, oranges, milk and beetroot. Potassium deficiency is rare as potassium is so widely found in the diet; but when it does occur it is very serious and can cause muscle weakness and cardiac arrest.

Sodium

Sodium is needed to control the body's fluid balance and maintain the heart's rhythm. A deficiency of sodium in the diet can cause low blood pressure. However, our diets are generally high in sodium and we are more likely to take in too much sodium, which can contribute to high blood pressure. Salt is the main source of sodium in our diet and it is found in processed foods and added to cooking and food as table salt. It is recommended that adults take in no more than four grams of salt a day, but it is thought that we take in much larger amounts, up to ten grams a day.

Salt is toxic to babies because their kidneys are not able to process it, and baby food is carefully controlled for levels of sodium.

FLUID INTAKE

In planning a healthy diet for children we must also take their fluid intake into consideration. Water is essential for life; humans can survive for up to eight weeks without food but only a few days without water. The body loses water daily though sweat, the excretion of urine and from chemical reactions in the body cells. An adult should take in two to three litres of water daily, of which at least two litres should come from beverages – the rest comes from our food.

Functions of water

- Vital to life – two-thirds of our body is water.
- Transports nutrients, oxygen, hormones and enzymes around the body.

❱ Transports waste products and carbon dioxide around the body.

❱ Quenches thirst.

❱ Provides the body with calcium and fluoride.

❱ Keeps the body cool.

Water intake must be increased when the child is ill (for example vomiting or diarrhoea) or after intense physical activity. Water intake must also be increased in hot weather as the body sweats more. If fluid intake is not increased at these times dehydration can result.

Dehydration

Dehydration can occur after a 2% loss of water. Signs of dehydration include:

❱ headaches

❱ muscle cramps

❱ feeling dizzy and light-headed

❱ having a dry or sticky mouth

❱ producing less urine and darker urine

❱ feeling thirsty – this is not an early warning sign

❱ negative mood.

Signs of extreme dehydration:

❱ not producing urine

❱ sleepiness

❱ sunken eyes

❱ sunken fontanelle in babies

❱ fainting.

Dehydration in children

If a child in your care shows any of the following symptoms of dehydration, you must summon medical assistance:

❱ not producing tears/dry eyes

❱ sunken eyes

❱ little or no urine output for eight hours

- dry skin that sags back into position slowly when pinched up into a fold
- dry mouth
- sunken soft spot on the top of an infant's head
- fast-beating heart
- blood in the stools or vomit
- diarrhoea or vomiting (in infants under two months old)
- listlessness and inactivity.

What kind of drinks should be offered to children?

Young babies should be given breast milk/formula milk. Cooled boiled water may be given if the baby is thirsty. This water should be taken from the tap: bottled water should not be used because some bottled water contains high levels of sodium, which is poisonous to babies. Babies can be given full-fat cow's milk after their first birthday. Do not give babies low-fat or skimmed milk as they need the essential fat-soluble vitamins that are found in full-fat milk.

Juice is high in sugar, so it should not be given to babies under six months, and only sparingly after that. Unsweetened juice can be given to children, but only with meals to limit the potential damage to their teeth.

Tea and coffee are not suitable for young children as they contain high levels of caffeine and tannin, a substance which interferes with iron absorption. Fizzy drinks, such as colas and lemonade, are all acidic and high in sugar and should not be given to young children.

FOOD ADDITIVES

Food additives are substances added to food in order to sweeten, preserve or improve the colour of food. In the European Union all food additives have to be judged safe by the European Scientific Committee on Food. Once the additive is approved it is given an E number and can be used in food sold in member states. Food additives are most commonly found in processed foods, soft drinks, chocolate and processed meats.

Do food additives cause hyperactivity?
In the 1970s Dr Ben Feingold claimed a link between food additives and hyper-activity in children. Research investigating this claim has had mixed results, but a 2007 Southampton University study did find a link between certain colourings and hyperactivity. It is currently recommended that children with a diagnosis of ADHD restrict their intake of additives (Dunne *et al.* 2009).

FACTORS THAT INFLUENCE THE DIET

Figure 5.2 Factors in food choices

Available resources and cost

Proximity to food outlets affects food choices. A family who lives a long distance from larger retail outlets may not have a wide choice of foods and may not be able to avail of pricing offers. *Growing Up in Ireland,* an ongoing study into the lives of children in Ireland, found that nine-year-old children who lived further from large food outlets had a worse diet than those who lived close to retail outlets (see Layte & McCroy 2008).

Cost is also a factor in food choice. For example, many supermarkets offer savings for customers who bulk-buy, but if consumers do not have the financial resources or access to supermarkets they may not be able to avail of these long-term savings.

Nutritional content

The nutritional content of food influences food selection. If children are on a special diet or have followed health education programmes such as *Food Dudes* they may be more inclined to select healthier food.

Sensory influences

Food choices are influenced by sensory factors such as the smell, colour and taste of the food. Children are more likely to want to eat food that has an attractive smell and colour and tastes good.

Psychological influences

'Special' food is often used as a reward or to celebrate events such as birthdays and weddings. The principles of conditioning and reinforcement mean that we associate certain foods (e.g. cake) with feelings of happiness. If we associate eating cake with feeling happy this can lead to a craving for cake. We may also associate food with negative effects and develop an aversion to the food. For example, how many of us associate flat 7-Up with being sick?

Religious beliefs and culture

The requirement to adhere to a certain diet and abstain from certain foods or to fast at certain times of the year is a feature of many world religions. It is the responsibility of the ECCE worker to find out if this affects any of the children in their care and to make adequate provision for these children.

Islam

Muslim children are required to abstain from pork and pork products, any fish without scales and any meat that is not killed in the way laid down by the Qur'an (the holy book of Islam). All children are to be breastfed until age two. Fasting is observed during the lunar month of Ramadan. During this time Muslims abstain from all food and drink between sunrise and sunset. Children under 12 years are exempt from observing Ramadan.

Judaism

Animals and birds must be slaughtered in accordance with Jewish law to be kosher (acceptable). Pork and shellfish are forbidden. Milk and meat must not be cooked or eaten together.

Hinduism

Orthodox Hindus are vegetarians because they believe in *ahimsa* – non-violence towards living things. Non-orthodox Hindus will not eat beef, because the cow is considered a sacred animal; or pork, because the pig is considered unclean.

THINK ABOUT IT

How can we meet the dietary requirements of children from different religions in an ECCE setting?

Allergies

A food allergy is an abnormal response of the immune system to an otherwise harmless food. According to the Irish Nutrition and Dietetic Institute (www.indi.ie), up to 5% of children and 3% of adults have food allergies. The most common food allergies are to:

▶ peanuts
▶ soya
▶ tree nuts such as almonds, walnuts
▶ wheat
▶ milk
▶ shellfish
▶ eggs
▶ fish.

Allergic reactions range in severity. The most common symptoms of an allergic reaction include itchy skin, hives, nausea, sore eyes and feeling faint.

The most severe allergic reaction is known as anaphylaxis, which involves several areas of the body and is life-threatening. Anaphylactic shock results in a raised pulse rate and impaired breathing. Emergency medical treatment should be sought at once if you suspect anaphylactic shock. A child with an allergy may have an adrenaline pen and if the child goes into anaphylactic shock this must be administered immediately.

Chronic conditions requiring special diets

As we discussed in Chapter Two, a chronic condition is one that is long term and cannot be cured but can be managed. Certain chronic conditions require dietary management and these include coeliac condition, diabetes, cystic fibrosis and lactose intolerance.

Coeliac condition

In coeliac disease the intestine has an abnormal response to gluten, a protein found in wheat, oats, rye and barley. If a coeliac eats gluten it will damage the small intestine as the body mistakenly perceives gluten as the enemy and attacks it. This causes the small intestine to become inflamed and unable to absorb nutrients properly.

Symptoms typical of coeliac disease are diarrhoea, constipation, weight loss, pot belly, mouth ulcers, fatigue, indigestion and stomach bloating. It is not known what causes coeliac disease.

What to do if you are caring for a child with coeliac disease: You must ensure that there are gluten-free alternatives available for the child. The child will not be able to eat wheat, so you will have to plan a wheat-free diet. You must also be aware that many processed foods, such as sausages and burgers, contain gluten: check whether the ones you are providing contain gluten. You can contact the Coeliac Society of Ireland for an up-to-date list of coeliac-friendly products. Further information is available at www.coeliac.ie. You must also be aware of the risk of cross-contamination when gluten-free foods come into contact with foods containing gluten. Different kitchen utensils must be used when preparing gluten-free food and food containing gluten.

Diabetes

Diabetes results from the body's inability to break down sugars in the bloodstream. There are two types of diabetes: type I is caused by the body's inability to produce insulin, the hormone that regulates glucose in the blood; type II diabetes, which is rare in children, is caused by poor diet and obesity.

What to do if you are caring for a child with diabetes: A child with diabetes may need a different diet, with no extra sugars. If the child is insulin dependent, ECCE workers may have to administer insulin to the child before/after meals.

Cystic fibrosis

As discussed in Chapter Two, cystic fibrosis is a genetic condition. The body produces a thick sticky mucus which it cannot break down. This mucus builds up and damages the internal organs, in particular the lungs and digestive system.

Dietary requirements for a child with cystic fibrosis: A child with cystic fibrosis will have to take certain vitamins and enzymes before meals in order to aid the digestion process. They will also require a higher-calorie diet as the mucus build-up in the small intestine reduces the body's ability to extract nutrients from food. Children with cystic fibrosis require 20% more calories and protein than other children.

PKU

Phenylketonuria (known as PKU) is a common metabolic disorder that affects many children in Ireland. In PKU the body cannot break down the amino acid phenylalanine. If the condition is undiagnosed, protein builds up in the brain, causing irreversible intellectual disability. Children must inherit a copy of the PKU gene from **both** parents in order to develop PKU. One in 35 Irish adults is a carrier of PKU and one in 4,500 Irish children have PKU. All children in Ireland are tested for PKU at birth when a sample of blood is taken from the child's heel. This is called the Guthrie test.

Treatment and dietary requirements: The damage caused by PKU is easily limited by following a special diet. A child with PKU will have to follow a diet low in phenylalanine for life, and will have to avoid protein-rich foods such as meat and milk. A dietician will design a special diet for parents and pre-school workers to follow.

Galactosaemia

Galactosaemia is a metabolic disorder common in Ireland. In galactosaemia the body cannot break down galactose, a sugar found in lactose. Galactosaemia affects one in 19,000 children born in Ireland and is most common among members of the Travelling community (one child in every 4,503). The Guthrie test also tests for galactosaemia.

Treatment and dietary requirements: Children who are diagnosed with galactosaemia will have to follow a special diet, as advised by a dietician, which will not include milk, butter, cheese and other dairy products. If left untreated galactosaemia can cause intellectual disability, cirrhosis of the liver and cataracts.

Lactose intolerance

This is the inability to absorb lactose, which is the main sugar found in milk. There are three types of lactose intolerance. Hereditary lactose intolerance is genetic – it runs in families; primary lactose intolerance is common among certain ethnic groups and is worse in childhood than in adulthood; secondary lactose intolerance is a side effect of certain conditions including Crohn's disease and coeliac disease. It is common in young children, as the enzyme the body uses to break down lactose has not yet matured, and often occurs in premature babies.

Foods that contain lactose include: milk (and milk powder), butter, yoghurt and cheese; bread and baked goods; chocolate; and various prepared foods.

The symptoms of lactose intolerance, which usually occur between 30 minutes and two hours after eating, include:

▶ wind
▶ stomach rumbling
▶ diarrhoea
▶ floating or foul-smelling stools
▶ nausea
▶ weight loss
▶ a bloated feeling.

The treatment for lactose intolerance will depend on the type of lactose intolerance. For those with hereditary lactose intolerance a completely lactose-free diet will be necessary. However, those with primary or secondary lactose intolerance may not have to eliminate lactose completely and may be able to follow a low-lactose diet. A dietician will devise a suitable diet in consultation with other healthcare professionals and parents.

EXERCISE

Devise a meal plan for a week for a pre-school child with coeliac condition or diabetes.

Focus on: Food and Nutrition Guidelines for Pre-school

In 2004 the Department of Health and Children published guidelines on the provision of food in pre-school services (DoHC 2004). The guidelines set out the requirements for provision of meals in a setting and are used by the Inspectorate team to asses the provision of food and nutrition by a service.

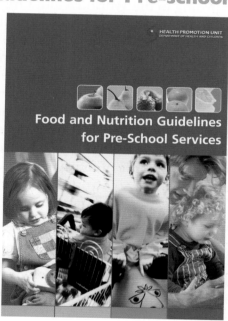

Food and Nutrition Guidelines for Pre-School Services

It is recommended that food should be offered to young children at least every three hours.

▶ **Children in full daycare (more than five hours):** Offer at least two meals and two snacks, for example breakfast, snack, lunch and snack. One meal should be a hot meal. If children are there for a long day, an evening meal may also need to be provided. If a main meal is not provided for some reason, ensure that parents know this so they can offer suitable meals at home.

▶ **Children in daycare for up to five hours per session:** Offer at least two meals and one snack, for example breakfast, snack and lunch. It is not necessary to serve a hot meal, but the meal should include at least one serving from each of the four main shelves of the food pyramid.

▶ **Children in daycare for up to 3.5 hours per session:** Offer one meal and one snack, for example, snack and lunch. This group may also include after-school care.

The guidelines also cover the provision of drinks and fluids. Water should be readily available throughout the day and children should be encouraged to drink up to six cups of fluid per day. Water for infants under 12 months should be boiled and cooled before use. Note that bottled water is not suitable as it can contain high levels of sodium.

CHILDHOOD OBESITY

According to the World Health Organisation (WHO), we are currently in the middle of a global obesity epidemic. It is thought that 17.6 million children worldwide are overweight. In 2005 the Department of Health and Children estimated that 30,000 Irish children were obese. Layte and McCroy (2008) found that 19% of nine-year-olds were overweight and 7% were obese. It was found that girls were more likely than boys to be overweight or obese. The 2012 *National Pre-School Nutrition Survey* (Walton 2012) found that one in four Irish pre-schoolers were overweight or obese. The survey sampled 500 Irish pre-schoolers aged between one and four years and found that 27% of two-year-olds were obese; this figure rose to 32% of three-year-olds but fell to 8% of four-year-olds.

THINK ABOUT IT

Why do you think childhood obesity is so high in Ireland? How can we try to combat childhood obesity?

What is the difference between being overweight and being obese?

▶ A child is **overweight** if they weigh 10–20% over the ideal weight for their age and height.
▶ A child is **obese** if they weigh 20% or more over the ideal weight for their age and height.

Indicators that a child may be overweight/obese is if the child's upper arms and thighs have rolls of fat that strain the sleeves and legs of clothes that otherwise fit well.

Causes of childhood obesity

- An **inappropriate diet** is the main cause of childhood obesity. An inappropriate diet is one high in foods from the top shelf of the food pyramid such as chocolate, crisps, fried foods and fizzy drinks. It could also be a diet made up of healthy foods but with inappropriate portion sizes. Children do not need portion sizes as large as adults' and should not be served adult portions.
- **Lack of exercise** is thought to be a major cause of childhood obesity. Increasingly children are living sedentary lives, spending more time watching TV and less time engaged in physical activity. This, combined with a diet high in calories and saturated fat, leads to weight gain.
- **Where children live:** the 2008 *Growing Up in Ireland* survey found that living in an area with fewer food outlets or fewer outlets selling affordable, high-quality food had a negative effect on dietary quality.

Effects of childhood obesity

Childhood obesity has far-reaching effects, both physical and psychosocial. Physically, obese children are less fit than their peers and may be unable to engage in physical education activities and sports. Overweight children are placing more pressure on their joints, which may lead to problems in adolescence and later life. Childhood obesity increases the child's risk of type II diabetes and is thought to increase the risk of asthma and make the child more prone to chest infections. Research also indicates a link between obesity and early puberty.

Some of the biggest effects of childhood obesity are psychosocial. Obese children are often a target for stigmatisation and discrimination and are more likely to be the victims or perpetrators of bullying. Obese children have also been found to have poorer social relationships and a narrower social network than non-obese children.

EXERCISE

If you are on placement in a pre-school where children bring in their own lunches, conduct an observational study on children's lunchboxes. Observe ten children at random to see what food they bring in every day and how it compares to the recommendations in the food pyramid. Then observe the children to see how much of the food they consume. You could make graphs to show your results.

Exercise pyramid

Just as there is a food pyramid to provide guidance for nutrition requirements, there is an exercise pyramid to offer guidance on how much exercise children should take. The HSE recommends that children should be active for at least 60 minutes every day of the week. Research indicates that Irish children do not currently get enough exercise; just over 50% of children exercise four or more times a week (Kelly *et al.* 2012). Exercise plays a key role in fighting obesity, but it is also essential for helping children and young people build strong bones and a strong cardiovascular system.

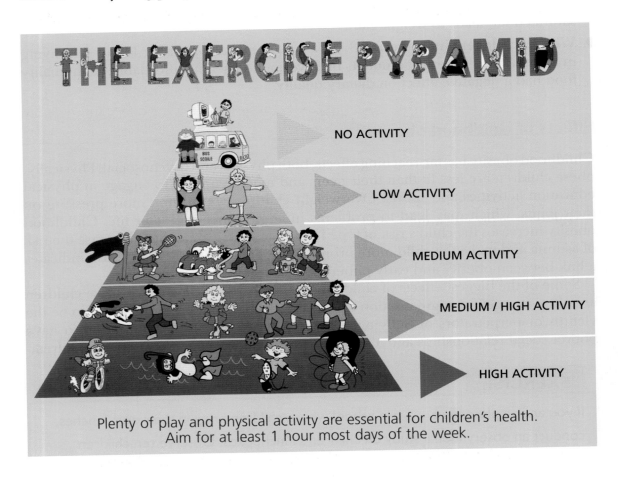

THE EXERCISE PYRAMID

NO ACTIVITY

LOW ACTIVITY

MEDIUM ACTIVITY

MEDIUM / HIGH ACTIVITY

HIGH ACTIVITY

Plenty of play and physical activity are essential for children's health.
Aim for at least 1 hour most days of the week.

THINK ABOUT IT

How can you ensure that the children in your setting get enough exercise every day?

MALNUTRITION

Malnutrition occurs when one or more nutrients are missing from the diet. This may be accompanied by **undernutrition**, which is when insufficient food is eaten. Malnutrition means literally 'bad nourishment' and is usually caused by one of three factors:

1 not enough food
2 too much food
3 eating the wrong type of food, e.g. a diet consisting solely of convenience and fast foods.

Malnutrition is a serious problem in the developing world; half of the deaths of children under five in the developing world are caused by malnutrition (WHO 2000). Protein deficiency malnutrition is most commonly found in Asia, followed by Africa, Latin America and the Caribbean.

Symptoms of malnutrition

▶ Tiredness and lack of energy.
▶ Failure to grow and gain weight.
▶ Low resistance to infection – the child may experience frequent colds and sore throat.
▶ Bleeding gums.
▶ Poor skin and hair condition.
▶ In extreme cases the body starts to experience marasmus, when body fat and tissue start to disintegrate.

Signpost for reflection

It is well documented that children learn from observing adult behaviour. With this in mind, reflect on your own diet. Make a record of what you eat on a typical day in college. How does this measure up to the healthy eating guidelines? What messages do your eating habits send to the children in your care?

chapter six

Safety in the ECCE Setting

LEARNING OUTCOMES

After reading this chapter you will be:

▶ familiar with the safety requirements for an ECCE setting

▶ aware of factors that pose a risk to the safety of young children

▶ able to identify risks and hazards and take steps to make an environment safe for young children

▶ familiar with fire safety, water safety, farm safety, car safety and road safety in relation to children.

INTRODUCTION

One of the questions parents ask when choosing a pre-school is 'Will my child be safe here?' Under the Child Care (Pre-School Services) (No. 2) Regulations 2006, pre-schools must provide a safe environment for the children in their care. As an ECCE worker it is your responsibility both to make sure that the centre you work in is safe for children and to prevent accidents. As anyone who has spent any time with young children knows, they can be prone to accidents.

▶ Young children are **curious** about the world around them and want to explore their environment. This can lead to unsafe situations when children's curiosity gets the better of them. For example, a child interested in water may attempt to explore a pond or stream and put themselves in danger of drowning.

▶ Young children have **no sense of danger** and do not have the knowledge or experience of the world to know what is dangerous. A young child does not realise that a hot kettle will burn them or that broken glass will cut them.

▶ Young children may be **over-confident** in their physical abilities and push themselves too far physically. For example, a young child may climb too high on a climbing frame and get stuck.

The responsibility for preventing accidents rests with the adults caring for children. Adults must assess the environment for hazards and risks to ensure children's safety and any potential hazards should be dealt with. It is often said that when you are caring for children you need eyes in the back of your head, and accidents are more likely to occur when adults are distracted or stressed and not paying enough attention to the children in their care. Accidents are also more likely to happen if there are not enough adults for the number of children in the setting. For this reason the adult:child ratio in ECCE settings is tightly regulated (see Chapter One).

Adults must also be mindful of their own behaviour and safety practices. Children copy adults' behaviour – if adults are poor role models and do not model good safety practices for children, accidents are likely to happen. For example, if adults do not look right and left when crossing the road, children may copy this behaviour and risk being involved in an accident.

Finally, it is important that children are exposed to **manageable** risk. As adults we can sometimes become overprotective and attempt to keep children from all risk. However, this is not always appropriate. Children *need* to be exposed to some level of risk in order to learn good safety practices, but this should be age-appropriate risk. For example, it is an age-appropriate risk for a pre-schooler to be encouraged to ride a bike or trike; it is not an age-appropriate risk for a pre-schooler to be encouraged to walk on the road by themselves.

LEGAL REQUIREMENTS

Under the Safety, Health and Welfare at Work Act 2005, all employers must assess the hazards and risks in their workplace and make appropriate plans to eliminate hazards and minimise risk. This is usually done by conducting a risk assessment of the setting and should be included in the safety statement.

Hazards and risks

▶ **Hazard:** something that could cause harm. For example, a window is a hazard if it is left open.
▶ **Risk:** the chance that harm might occur. For example, what is the risk that the window *will* be left open, thus creating a hazard?

Hazards can result from wear and tear, vandalism, accidental damage, the weather and human error. It is our responsibility as ECCE workers to limit the occurrence of hazards by checking materials in the setting every day. The following daily checks should be performed.

- **Plastic** materials, including toys, should be checked for cracks and sharp edges.
- **Metal** materials should be checked for rust and chipped paint.
- **Wooden** materials should be checked for splinters and frayed edges.
- **Fabric** materials should be checked for fraying edges and to see if they are becoming threadbare.

The results of these daily checks should be documented. Any materials that become hazardous should be removed from the setting.

Checks in the outdoor area

All settings are required to have access to an outdoor play area. This area should also be checked daily.

- Fences and gates should be fastened shut.
- Check for pests and vermin.
- Outdoor equipment should be cleaned and checked for damage.
- Sand areas should be covered at the end of the day and when not in use.
- Any plants in the outdoor area must be checked to make sure that they are not poisonous.

ACCIDENTS

Accidents are a common childhood experience. In 2009, 4,367 children aged between one and four and 972 babies were hospitalised as a result of accidental injury (Brooks *et al.* 2010), and 17% of three-year-olds have attended hospital as a result of accidental injury (ESRI & TCD: *Growing Up in Ireland* 2011). There are five main categories of accident that the children in your care may experience.

1 Falls and cuts.
2 Burns and scalds.
3 Choking, suffocation, strangulation.
4 Poisoning.
5 Drowning.

Falls and cuts

All children trip and fall from time to time. Most of these falls are minor, but some will be more serious. Accidental falls made up 41.6% of the hospitalisations for accidental injury in 2009 (Brooks *et al.* 2010). Falls are a perfectly normal aspect of development but should be kept to a minimum.

Table 6.1 Falls and cuts: risks and prevention

Hazard	Risk	Prevention
Unlocked windows	Child falls out of the window	Fit locks on all windows
Baby walkers	Baby walkers can affect children's depth perception, so there is a risk of the child falling over a step while in the baby walker	Baby walkers should not be used around open steps and should only be used under supervision
Unguarded stairs	Child falls down the steps	Fit stair gates at the top and bottom of all stairs to prevent children gaining access
Toys loose on floor	Child/adult trips over toys	Pick up toys as necessary throughout the day
Climbing frames	Child falls when climbing	Climbing frames are a suitable activity for older children only Pre-schoolers should not have access to climbing frames
Knives	Child cuts themselves	Keep out of the reach of children
Sharp edges and corners on furniture	Child runs into sharp corners/edges	Fit plastic corner covers on any sharp edges

Burns and scalds

Children's skin is thinner than adults' skin, so burns and scalds are more serious for children – and they are potentially fatal for young children. Burns and scalds are most likely to happen in the kitchen. This risk should be eliminated in the ECCE setting by keeping children out of the kitchen. Hot drinks are a major hazard around children; any hot drink can scald a baby even 15 minutes after it's been made.

Children should wear a high sun protection factor (SPF) sunscreen on sunny days and in summer to prevent sunburn. You should take an occupational first aid course as part of your training to teach you how to treat burns and scalds.

Table 6.2 Burns and scalds: risks and prevention

Hazard	Risk	Prevention
Kettle on countertop Saucepan on the edge of the cooker hob	Child pulls the kettle/ saucepan down on top of themselves	Keep kettles and saucepans out of reach of children Use the cooker's back rings for saucepans Keep children out of the kitchen Turn saucepan handles in
Hot drink on edge of table or countertop	Child pulls the cup down on top of themselves	Children should not be able to reach hot drinks No hot drinks in the main rooms of the setting
Hot day	Sunburn	Apply sun cream Keep children in shade Make sure they wear a hat
Hot radiators	Child touches the radiator	Fit thermostatic valves on taps and radiators Fit radiator covers
Faulty electrical equipment	Electric burns	Regularly check equipment for faults
Open fire in main living area	Child falls into the fire	Open fires should not be used in ECCE settings Use fireguards in the home
Adult smoking cigarettes	Child picks up the cigarette and is burned	Adults should not smoke around children

Choking, suffocation, strangulation

Asphyxia occurs when the airway is blocked, preventing air leaving and entering the lungs. This can result from a foreign body being lodged in the airway (choking), because the mouth or nose is blocked (suffocation) or because the airway is blocked (strangulation). Young children are at high risk of all three.

Choking

Young children are learning how to regulate their eating. They may gulp their food or they may not chew their food properly. Some foods are not suitable for small children because they are a significant choking hazard. These include peanuts, popcorn and sausages (which can slip down the throat).

As you will learn in your Child Development module, young children learn through their senses. This is why you often see young children, especially babies and toddlers, put everything into their mouth. Because of this, choking can be a significant hazard for young children. You must be careful to provide toys that do not have small pieces, which a child could swallow and choke on.

Suffocation

Pillows and duvets are not suitable for babies under one year old as they do not have the strength or dexterity to pull the duvet off their face if they wriggle underneath it. Plastic bags should be kept out of reach of children and should never be given to children as a plaything.

Strangulation

Ribbons or clothes tied too tightly around a child's neck may present a risk of strangulation. Children should never be put to sleep with ribbons around their neck as they can get tangled. Blind cords which can form a loop present a strangulation risk for children. In recent years, five children have died in Ireland as a result of strangulation from blind cords (*Irish Times* 2012). This has led to the publication of new standards for blind cords in Ireland.

Poisoning

Because children learn through their senses they are also at risk of ingesting food or liquid that is poisonous. Cleaning materials or medication are the biggest poisoning risk for young children and should be packaged with a childproof lock. However, older children are capable of opening containers that have a childproof lock. Children should **never** have access to cleaning materials or medication in the setting. They should always be kept out of children's reach in a locked press or cabinet. At home, cleaning materials and medication should always be kept in their original container so that children (or adults) do not mistake the material for a non-toxic fluid. If children in your care do ingest a poison, contact the National Poisons Bureau helpline for advice. In 2009, 340 children were hospitalised due to accidental poisoning (Brooks *et al.* 2010).

Drowning

On average 150 people drown in Ireland every year (Irish Water Safety website). Children, especially very young children, are at a high risk of drowning. A child can drown in five centimetres (two inches) of water because they may not have the upper body strength to pull themselves up if they fall into water. Children should not be left unsupervised in the bath until they are six years old and should not be left to bathe with the door closed until late childhood. Baths should never be left full of water. If the home has a paddling pool it should only be used with parental supervision. It is important to teach children the principles of water safety to prepare them for swimming in a swimming pool or the sea.

Water safety when swimming

▶ Children should be encouraged to learn how to swim. Knowing how to swim is the best way of promoting water safety.

▶ Children or adults should never swim alone in case they get into difficulties. Only swim in areas that are attended by a lifeguard who is trained in life saving. Never swim when tired.

▶ Do not swim until one hour after eating.

▶ Do not swim in strange places where you are unfamiliar with riptides and currents that can pull you out to sea.

▶ Never swim out to sea: you could get out of your depth. Instead, swim parallel to shore, where you will not get out of your depth.

▶ Air mattresses and lilos are easily caught in currents and should not be used in open water.

SAFETY AT HOME

When a new baby is born the home must be adapted to make it a safe environment for the growing child. Parents will have to take some time assessing the home for hazards and taking steps to prevent hazards. This is often referred to as 'baby proofing' the home. This process should be completed before the baby is born and revised in line with the baby's growing abilities.

Preventing accidents in the home

Babies and children must be supervised at all times: all the safety equipment in the world is useless if adults are not vigilant with regard to child safety. The floor and stairs must be kept obstruction-free to prevent children (and adults) falling over items. Babies must never be left unattended on raised surfaces as they may roll or crawl off the edge. Young children must never be left alone in the bath as they can easily slip under the water and may not have the upper body strength to pull themselves back up again. The following safety equipment is necessary to help keep children safe in the home.

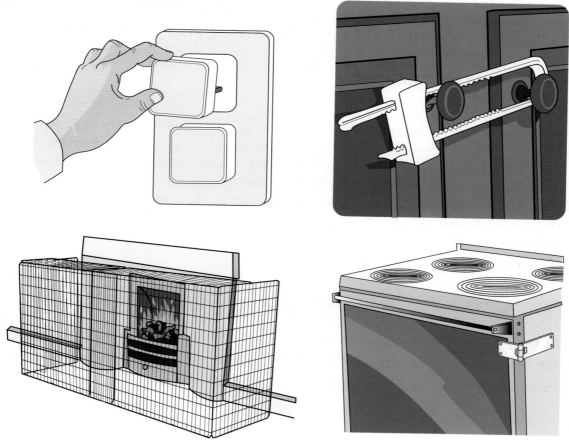

Figure 6.1 Safety equipment for the home

Smoke detectors are an essential piece of equipment for every household. If there is an open fire or range in the home a **fire guard** will be an essential purchase to prevent children (or careless adults!) burning themselves. **Socket covers** will be needed to plug any open electrical sockets, preventing children from sticking their fingers into the sockets and getting an electric shock. Young children cannot negotiate stairs successfully in an adult-like fashion until they are four years old (Flood 2010b). Therefore, any home with stairs or steps will need a **stair gate**. Stair gates should be fitted at the top and bottom of the stairs to prevent children from accessing the stairs unsupervised. If a high chair is being used, a **harness** should be used to strap the child in safely and securely. Any windows the child can reach by themselves or by climbing on furniture must be fitted with **window locks**. Cupboards that contain dangerous or delicate materials should be fitted with **cupboard locks** to limit children's access. Children can learn to open cupboard locks with practice, so any poisonous materials, such as cleaning materials and bleach, should be kept **locked away** and **at a height** children cannot reach. The bath should be fitted with a **non-slip bath mat** to prevent children slipping and falling when getting out of the bath.

CASE STUDY: BABY WALKERS

Baby walkers are associated with more injuries than any other type of nursery equipment. They allow babies to move quickly and raise them to a height where they can reach for items that are normally out of reach. They also interfere with children's depth perception, which means that they cannot judge distances. In 2002, 2,350 babes were taken to hospital in England after being injured using a baby walker (Child Accident Prevention Trust). Following a 2005 EU directive, baby walkers now move more slowly and are designed to stop if one wheel goes over a step.

EXERCISE: SPOT THE DIFFERENCE – HOME SETTING

Below are two pictures of a kitchen. One picture contains several safety hazards, the other does not. Examine each picture and identify the hazards present. You can then make suggestions as to how these hazards can be removed.

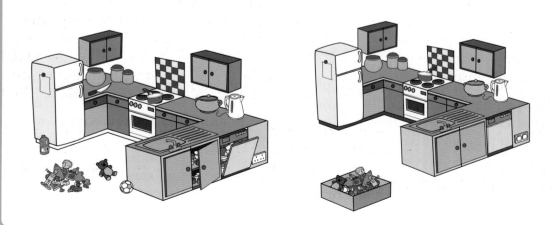

EXERCISE: SPOT THE DIFFERENCE – PRE-SCHOOL SETTING

Below are two pictures of the main room in a pre-school. One picture contains several safety hazards, the other does not. Examine each picture and identify the hazards present. You can then make suggestions as to how these hazards can be prevented.

SECURITY ARRANGEMENTS IN A PRE-SCHOOL

All ECCE settings must have comprehensive security arrangements in place to protect children. Good security arrangements are essential for a number of reasons. If parents see that a pre-school has well-thought-out security arrangements they will feel reassured that their child will be safe and well cared for. Good security arrangements safeguard children and help the childcare worker to keep children safe, both by keeping the children in the centre and by controlling the outsiders who have access to the centre. By controlling who has access to the setting the ECCE worker can ensure the safety of all children. Good security arrangements are also a sign of a quality centre that cares about the safety and security of the children in its care.

Security is also a legal requirement: under the Child Care (Pre-School Services) (No. 2) Regulations (2006) (DoHC 2006) an ECCE setting must have good security arrangements. Figure 6.1 illustrates some security procedures that should be considered by ECCE settings.

Figure 6.2 Security arrangements in a pre-school

Doors/gates that lock

Doors and gates in an ECCE setting must lock, and lock at a height the children cannot reach. If doors are unlocked children may wander out of the building without adult supervision; and if door handles are at a height children can reach, they may attempt to unlock the doors, especially older pre-schoolers who have the dexterity to undo bolts.

Fingerprint scan/fob in/intercom system

Many settings are now embracing new technology to secure the safety of the children in their care. Staff are given a fob that they use to swipe in and out and open the entrance door of the setting. Only those with a fob can enter the building freely; all other visitors, including parents, have to press the intercom and wait to be buzzed in by a staff member. This removes the risk of any unauthorised person gaining access to the setting. Some settings use fingerprint scanning technology, which uses each person's individual fingerprint to scan them in. This technology is very effective, but installing and maintaining the system can be very expensive.

Photo identification

When parents register their children with a childcare setting they must nominate a list of people authorised to collect the child. Many settings will require photo identification to accompany this list for identification purposes.

Password system

Settings may also operate a password system whereby the parents/guardians of each child nominate a password that must be given to staff by the person collecting the child. Each child has a unique password, which should only be shared with people the parents/guardians trust to collect their child. A password system works very well as a precaution if someone who does not usually collect the child comes to the setting. Once the password is given staff can be reassured that it is safe to hand over the child to this person.

Signing in and out

Under the Child Care (Pre-School Services) (No.2) Regulations 2006, all adults and children who enter and leave the premises must sign in and out. This means that if there is an emergency evacuation, an exact list of who is in the premises is available. When the HSE Inspectorate team comes to inspect a setting they can ask to see this record.

Garda vetting of staff/students/volunteers

Under the Child Care (Pre-School Services) (No.2) Regulations 2006, all staff, students and volunteers in an ECCE setting must obtain Garda clearance before commencing employment, placement or volunteering with the service. This supports best practice for child protection (DoHC 1999, 2002). Currently legislation is before the Oireachtas to make it a legal requirement that everyone working with children and vulnerable people are Garda vetted. Failure by employers to do so will be a criminal offence.

Morning meet and greet: points to remember

Greet each child and their parent/guardian each day. Greet the child individually and ask how they are that morning. This helps the child to feel secure and welcome in the setting. It also reassures the carer who is leaving the child that their child will be well cared for in their absence. If the parent/guardian is unfamiliar, make sure to check the password and/or photo identification. Note that carers can only take a child from a guardian who is aged 16 or over.

This system should ensure the security and safety of all children in the setting. However, if the worst happens and a child goes missing, the following steps should be taken.

1 Inform the supervisor of what has happened. The supervisor will then inform the child's parents and the Garda Síochána.

2 Make sure all the other children are safe. Gather the children together and nominate a staff member to stay with them while other staff members search for the missing child. The staff member staying with the other children should organise an absorbing activity to distract them from the unfolding crisis. Staff members should be prepared to reassure children as necessary.

3 Start a systematic search from where the child was last seen and check external exits to ascertain whether the child left through one of them. Get down to the child's level to try to figure out if anything may have attracted their attention.

EXERCISE

Happy Feet is a sessional service catering for 15 children between the ages of three and five. Happy Feet is run by Maureen and Susan, both of whom have been working in childcare for over ten years. Maureen has an NCVA Certificate in Childcare (equivalent to FETAC Level 5). Susan holds some additional certificates and is thinking about going back to college to complete her full Level 5 award.

There are some health and safety issues in the setting:

▶ The table top and block areas get very messy during the course of the day.
▶ Some of the toys in the table-top area and block area are old – the last stock update was four years ago.
▶ The outdoor area backs on to a local park. On Monday mornings the staff often find empty beer cans and chip papers thrown over the wall.
▶ There is a crab apple tree in the corner of the outdoor play area.
▶ Some of the books have seen better days – a lot of the pages are dog-eared.
▶ There is a new child in the setting who is visually impaired.
▶ It is an old building, which can be draughty in winter.

1 Make a list of potential hazards in the setting and how these could be prevented or overcome.

2 If you were an HSE inspector, which areas would you be particularly concerned about?

FIRE SAFETY

Fire can spread quickly and is deadly to both children and adults. Fire poses a double hazard: smoke inhalation and burns. Of the two, smoke inhalation poses a more immediate threat; carbon monoxide poisoning can cause death within minutes.

Three things are needed for a fire to develop: oxygen, heat and fuel. These are represented in a triangle known as the fire triangle.

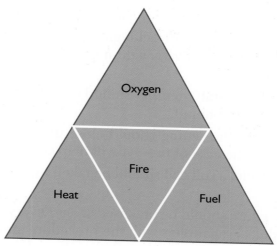

Figure 6.3 The fire triangle

All pre-schools must have a fire safety policy in place. Fire can break out at any time and will cause panic, so workers and children must all be prepared and know what to do in case of emergency. All ECCE workers should be trained in fire safety. Every room in the setting should have a smoke alarm and the batteries should be checked regularly. Smoke alarms should be tested at least once a week to make sure they are in working order. Fire blankets and fire extinguishers should be available, especially in the kitchen. Fire extinguishers must be serviced once a year to ensure that they are working correctly. Candles should be banned in the setting as these pose a fire hazard. Many fires are caused by electrical appliances overheating or by faulty electrical appliances. All electrical appliances should be unplugged when not in use and any faulty electrical appliances should be replaced.

Evacuation procedure

The setting should have an evacuation procedure in case of fire, and everyone must know what to do in an emergency. Staff must act quickly and calmly to secure and reassure all the children in their care.

▶ Each setting should have a designated safe area to go to in the event of an evacuation. All staff, work experience students and volunteers should be aware of the designated area. In an evacuation, staff must take the children to this area as quickly and calmly as possible.

▶ A designated person must be appointed to take the roll book and sign-in sheet so that a roll call can be taken in the designated area to ensure all children and adults are safe.

▶ When leaving the setting the group should leave in single file with one staff member at the front and one at the back. All belongings should be left behind (except the roll book and sign-in sheet). The evacuation should be conducted calmly and at walking pace.

▶ Before exiting the setting a staff member should check the toilets to ensure that no child or adult has been left behind.

▶ The last person to leave the setting should close the door behind them. This is especially important in the case of fire – it will help contain the blaze.

▶ Once everyone is outside, a roll call should be taken to make sure all children and staff are safe.

▶ The evacuation procedure should be practised at least every three months to ensure that children and adults are familiar with the procedure and confident about what to do in case of an emergency evacuation. Remember, children learn by repetition!

▶ During the practice drill, children should be reassured and praised. Remember to thank them for their help.

▶ After the drill, plan an absorbing activity to get the children to settle down.

Fire safety in the home

▶ **Fit a working smoke alarm:** A working smoke alarm should be fitted on each floor of the house. The alarm should be tested regularly to ensure that it is working, and the battery should be changed regularly.

▶ **Plan a fire escape route:** How many of us have planned our escape route in case of a fire in our home? Most fires happen at night and the combination of darkness and smoke from the fire will make familiar surroundings seem strange. As a family, sit down and plan the escape route, make sure every member of the family is aware of what to do and practise the route regularly to ensure familiarity. Make sure to have one or more back-up routes in case the route you have chosen is blocked by fire.

▶ **Check for fire hazards:** Households should check for and remove fire hazards as they arise. For example, turn off unused cooker rings, ensure the spark guard is covering the fire and ensure that fraying plugs are dealt with.

▶ **'Last thing at night' routine:** There should be a 'last thing at night routine' when you check for and deal with potential fire hazards. Make sure a fire guard covers an open fire, and that all exits are clear. Do not leave electrical devices on standby and ensure that all electrical items, e.g. mobile phone chargers, are unplugged. If there is a smoker in the house make sure they empty their ashtray and if candles are in use make sure they are well quenched before going to bed. Make it part of the nightly routine and it will become second nature!

ROAD SAFETY

Road traffic accidents cause one-fifth of all child injury-related deaths in the EU each year (WHO 2008). Children are more vulnerable to road traffic accidents as their smaller size can make them harder for drivers to spot. Inadequate supervision of children who have not developed the cognitive ability to judge a dangerous situation is also a major factor. Children must be taught the rules of the road in order to reduce the risk of road traffic accidents.

▶ Always cross the road at a pedestrian crossing and wait for the green man before you cross the road.

▶ Never cross the road between parked cars as this will make it more difficult for drivers to see you.

▶ When walking on country roads, wear a reflective arm belt or jacket.

▶ Children under the age of 12 should not be allowed to cross the road by themselves as they cannot yet judge the distance and speed of oncoming vehicles.

The Safe Cross Code is a fun and easy way to teach children the rules of the road.

1, 2, 3, Safe Cross,

4, 5, 6, Safe Cross,

1, 2, 3, 4, 5, 6, Safe Cross Code!

Remember, **One** look for a safe place

Two, don't hurry, stop and wait,

Three, look all around and listen before you cross the road,

Remember, **Four**, let all the traffic pass you,

Five, then walking straight across you,

Six, keep watching,

that's the **Safe Cross Code**!

Road Safety Week is held in October every year. This is a great opportunity to talk to children about road safety and to teach them the Safe Cross Code.

THINK ABOUT IT

What other activities could you plan for Road Safety Week?

CAR SAFETY

Between 1997 and 2004 30% of children who died in road accidents in Ireland were not wearing seatbelts or restraints. Under EU law all children who weigh less than 36kg or are under 150cm in height must use a car seat, booster seat or booster cushion when travelling in a car. Failure to do so puts the child in danger, and statistics show that using an appropriate car seat can reduce road injuries by between 60% and 90%. If you are transporting a child in your car it is your responsibility to make sure that they are using the appropriate restraints and seat. Failure to do so carries four penalty points and an €800 fine. It is important to pick a car seat in accordance with a child's *weight* and *height*, **not** their age.

Table 6.3 Car restraints for children

Rear-facing baby seat	Forward-facing car seat	Booster seat	Booster cushion
For babies up to 13kg (29lb)	For toddlers weighing 9–18kg (20–40lb)	For children weighing 15–25kg (33–35lb)	For children weighing 22–36kg (48–79lb)
Suitable from birth to 12–15 months	Suitable for children aged 9 months to 4 years	Suitable for children aged 4–6	Suitable for children aged 6–11/12
A rear-facing seat provides the best protection for the baby's head and neck, so it should be used for as long as possible	*The child should only move to a forward-facing car seat when they become too heavy or too tall for a rear-facing seat*		

Parents should take care when buying a car seat, booster seat or booster cushion. Car seats must always be bought new – the safety history of a second-hand seat cannot be verified. The equipment should only be bought from reputable sellers who provide guidance on how to install the seat. Three-quarters of car seats are not fitted correctly and this can lead to injury or death in an accident. The Road Safety Authority (RSA) runs Check it Fits road shows, where experts will check fitted car seats to make sure that they are safe. Car seats must always be replaced after a car accident, even if they do not look damaged, as they may have faults that are invisible to the naked eye.

TOY SAFETY

Every child loves toys and spends many hours playing with their favourites. Because of this, the manufacture of toys is strictly regulated. A **toy** is defined as product designed for play and used by children under the age of 14; toys include dolls, teddy bears, building blocks and toy cars. A **plaything** is a product not designed for play; playthings include sports equipment and jewellery.

All toys sold in Ireland must have a safe design and be made with non-toxic materials. Toys that meet these requirements will carry the CE mark, which means that they comply with European safety standards. Some products may also carry the EN71 mark (another EU safety mark) or the Kitemark (the UK safety symbol). *A Guide to Toy Safety*, published by the National Consumer Agency (NCA), outlines the following basic safety guidelines that toy manufacturers must follow.

▶ Toys should be made of materials which will not easily catch fire.

▶ Toys should be made of non-toxic materials.

▶ Folding toys and toys with hinges must be designed so that they will not trap fingers.

▶ Toys should be made so that moveable parts cannot escape.

▶ Toys with tubes, bars or levers should have protection against cutting.

▶ Toys must be strong and sturdy.

▶ Any removable pieces must be big enough that children cannot swallow them.

As an ECCE worker you should ask yourself the following questions when choosing toys.

▶ Is the toy **strong and sturdy** enough to deal with the rough and tumble of play?

▶ Is the toy **fire-proof** and **non-flammable**?

▶ Are there any **sharp edges**?

▶ Are there **small pieces**?

▶ Is the seller of the toy a **reputable seller**? Is there a **guarantee** on the toy?

▶ Is the toy **suitable** for the child for whom you are purchasing it?

▶ Is the toy **age-appropriate**? Check the recommended age on the toy's packaging. Do not buy a toy meant for an older child for a younger child – it may have small pieces that represent a choking hazard for the younger child. You should also consider whether the toy is suitable for younger children in the setting who may have access to the toy.

EXERCISE

In groups, take a trip to your nearest toy shop. Make a note of the most popular toys and what safety marks they carry. You could repeat this exercise at home and in your work experience setting. You could make a poster to show your findings.

PLANNING AN OUTING

Outings can be a great part of the early years curriculum. Outings help to make children aware of the world around them and promote the centre's links to the community (Standard 16 in Síolta). Outings can also be an excellent learning experience for children, giving them experiences that they cannot get inside the setting and complementing learning that takes place inside the setting. For example, on an outing to a petting farm or zoo children can see animals in real life as well as reading about them in story time.

However, taking pre-schoolers on an outing requires a lot of planning and care from a health and safety perspective. You will be taking children into a strange environment where they may feel nervous and overwhelmed. You and your co-workers will be in charge of the children and are responsible for making sure they have a fun and safe day. Before children or workers leave on the outing many hours of planning and preparation will be done to ensure that it runs smoothly. ECCE workers must consider the factors shown in Figure 6.4.

Figure 6.4 Planning an outing

Learning outcomes

Outings outside the setting can be a great learning experience for children. For example, on a trip to a pet farm children will learn the names of the animals and what they do, and about life on the farm. Learning outcomes should be planned in relation to developmental outcomes and Aistear.

Adult:child ratio

For a full-time pre-school service with children aged from three to six years the adult:child ratio is 1:8. However, if the group goes on an outing from the setting this ratio must be increased to one adult for every three children (1:3). Settings can make up the shortfall by recruiting parent volunteers or students on work placement, but they must be Garda vetted before they can accompany the children.

Parental permission

Signed parental permission must be received for each child before the outing. If a child does not have parental permission to go on the outing they cannot go on the trip.

The permission slip should be sent out to parents in good time before the trip and parents should be informed where the children are going, for how long and whether there are any special requirements for the day, e.g. if they will need special clothing or a packed lunch.

Transport

If transport is needed for the outing it must be planned in advance. If children are travelling by bus the bus must be fitted with seat belts for each child. If public transport is used, children must be supervised getting on, during the trip and getting off the transport.

First aid and medical needs

A fully stocked first aid kit must be taken on all outings and at least one first aider must be present. If any of the children are on any long-term medication, for example asthma inhalers, this must be brought on the outing in case it is needed. Medication can only be administered if parents have given the setting written permission to do so.

Food and drink

According to the *Food and Nutrition Guidelines for Pre-School Services* (DoHC 2004), children in full-time day care must be given two meals and two snacks during the course of the day. If children are on an outing these meals/snacks must be provided on the outing. Childcare providers must decide whether they will provide these or eat out. Any meals/snacks must be nutritionally balanced and any allergies or dietary requirements catered for. Drinks must always be brought on the outing.

Cost

The outing must be priced and budgeted for in advance. Settings must decide whether or not they will subsidise the outing. Remember, costs will need to be kept as low as possible for both the setting and the parents.

Weather conditions

In Ireland the weather will be unpredictable, so providers should plan for every eventuality. Sun hats and sun cream should be brought as well as rain jackets.

EXERCISE

In groups, plan an outing for a group of ten pre-schoolers aged four to five. Consider all safety concerns and how they will be met, and set learning outcomes.

CASE STUDY: PLANNING AN OUTING TO A LOCAL PARK

It is spring, and Happy Feet pre-school is planning an outing to the local park. Ten children attend the service and all have been given permission to attend. Maureen, the pre-school leader, is currently planning for the trip. Maureen regularly plans outings for the children. She feels it is important to bring the children out and make them familiar with their community (Standard 16 of Síolta). Maureen has chosen the local park for the outing as it links to her theme of the week, which is 'Spring'. Maureen has planned for the following learning outcomes.

▶ **Physical:** Gross motor skills and exercise.
▶ **Intellectual:** Active learning about flowers and trees; link to circle and story time activities.
▶ **Language:** Learning the names of flowers and trees in a real-life context.
▶ **Emotional:** Expending energy and releasing tension.

All four themes in Aistear will be met in the outing.

Maureen has recruited the work experience student Lena and two parent volunteers to accompany her on the trip in order to be compliant with the 1:3 ratio needed for outings. She has prepared the first aid kit and checked the child records for any allergies or medication that children are on. Permission slips were distributed to all parents one week prior to the outing and all parents agreed to the trip. Parents will be sent a text message the night before the trip in order to remind them to dress children appropriately for the outing and to send a packed lunch if required.

Farms and animals

Outings to farms are great learning opportunities for children. Children can encounter and pet animals that they do not usually experience. However, farms can be dangerous places for children. Between 1996 and 2009, 43 children were killed in accidents on Irish farms (HSA 2010). The most common accidents were crush injuries from heavy vehicles, injuries from farm machinery, and drowning in tanks, slurry pits and water troughs. Farm animals also present a hazard for children – there is a risk of animal bites and diseases that can be passed to humans.

All these hazards are preventable and an outing to the farm does represent a fun and enjoyable learning opportunity for children. If the ECCE worker plans properly for the visit and prepares the children for the rules of the farm there is no reason why the visit cannot be both fun and safe.

Before the visit

- **Clothes:** Make sure the children wear suitable clothes. Wellies or strong shoes should be worn as they are sturdy enough for walking over uneven ground and will keep feet dry in case of rain or walking through puddles!
- **Cuts and grazes:** Make sure any cuts or grazes are covered with waterproof dressings to prevent germs and bacteria entering the wound.
- **Allergies:** Check with the parents whether any children are allergic to animals. If they are, make sure that they do not have contact with the animals.
- **Supervision:** Plan for adequate supervision: make sure the adult:child ratio is appropriate and that all adults are aware of the rules of the trip.
- **Hand washing:** Speak to the children before the trip about the importance of hand washing after petting the animals as bacteria can be easily spread in this way. Similarly, explain to children that they are not to touch the animal's feed or litter trays.
- **Feeing animals:** Animals should be fed only with the permission of the owner; if you feed animals without the owner's permission you may feed the animal a substance that is toxic for them. There is also a risk of children being bitten while feeding the animals.
- **Pregnant staff:** Pregnant staff members should stay away from sheep or newborn lambs as they can pass on certain infections which are dangerous for pregnant women.

PETS IN THE ECCE SETTING

Some settings may decide to keep pets. These enhance children's experience and teach them the skills of caring for others and taking responsibility. This links to the following learning goals in Aistear:

- ‘Respect themselves and the environment’ (Well-being 1,5).
- ‘Respect life – their own and others’ – and know that life has a meaning and purpose’ (Well-being 4,5).
- ‘Be active citizens’ (Well-being 4,6).
- ‘Interact, work co-operatively and help others’ (Identity and Belonging 3,3).
- ‘Learn about the natural environment and its features, materials, animals and plant and their own responsibility as carers’ (Exploring and Thinking 1,3).

Focus on toxoplasmosis

Toxoplasmosis is an infection caused by the parasite *Toxoplasma gondii*, which is found in meat and animal faeces.

Effects of toxoplasmosis: Toxoplasmosis causes mild flu-like or prolonged glandular fever-type symptoms and is usually not dangerous for adults or children. However, toxoplasmosis is very dangerous if contracted by pregnant women as it can have a serious effect on the unborn child. If the mother becomes infected in early pregnancy she may miscarry or have a stillbirth. If the infection is contracted between the third and sixth month of pregnancy it can lead to the child developing hydrocephalus, brain lesions or eye damage.

Prevention: Good hygiene will help prevent toxoplasmosis. Litter boxes should be cleaned every day. Pregnant employees must never clean litter boxes. Gloves and aprons should be worn by all employees when changing litter boxes and hands must be washed after changing the box.

Animals pose safety risks, including the risks of falling over the animal, bites, allergies and infection. Some animals can be a source of human infection and the risks of keeping pets in a setting must be carefully deliberated before buying a pet. Infection can be spread from animals to humans by bacteria from sucking fingers after petting animals or eating food with which animals have had contact. Reptiles such as iguanas, lizards and turtles are particularly unsuitable for an ECCE setting as they carry a high risk of salmonella. The following guidelines should be followed when caring for pets in an ECCE setting.

- Animals that are kept in the setting must be in good health. Make sure any necessary inoculations have been administered and are up to date. Take the pet to the vet for regular check-ups to ensure that it is in good health.

- Children must be taught how to handle animals correctly and taught not to pull their ears or handle them roughly. Even the most placid animal may snap if it is continually handled roughly.
- Pets cannot be allowed to wander freely around the setting; they should be kept in a secure area.
- Animal feed and bowls must be kept out of the reach of children.
- Children must be taught to wash their hands before and after handling animals. This rule must be rigidly enforced.

VARIABLE WEATHER

As we're all aware, Ireland is prone to variable weather conditions! Some people say that in Ireland you can experience all four seasons in one day. ECCE settings must be prepared for this. Many ECCE settings will ask parents to pack a raincoat and/ or wellingtons each day. This is a great idea as it means that children can go outside whatever the weather. In the winter months parents should be asked to pack hats and scarves and to dress children appropriately so that they can still experience outdoor play. Settings may hold a supply of salt in case of ice so that they can keep the path to the setting safe in icy conditions. If the outdoor area is iced over, do not bring the children outside in case of accidents. However, on the rare occasions when it snows, make sure to wrap the children up and go outside to experience the wonder that is falling snow!

POLICIES AND PROCEDURES

Using the guiding principles of legislation and good practice, an ECCE centre will devise a range of policies and procedures to maintain a safe setting, including a safety policy and an accident policy. You can read more about these and other polices needed for ECCE settings in the next chapter.

Signpost for reflection

Some people argue that we are now overprotective of our children. Do you think this is true? What are the advantages and disadvantages of protecting our children from hazards in the environment?

Section Three

HEALTH PROMOTION

chapter seven

Promoting a Healthy Environment in an ECCE Setting

After reading this chapter you will be able to:

▶ identify the routes of infection

▶ promote good hygiene measures in an ECCE setting

▶ explain the benefits of hand washing

▶ promote a healthy environment in the ECCE setting

▶ sterilise children's feeding equipment

▶ identify the benefits of rest and sleep for children

▶ discuss risk factors and prevention measures for sudden infant death syndrome (SIDS)

▶ develop policies and procedures to promote a healthy ECCE environment.

INTRODUCTION

In the previous chapter we discussed how to keep children physically safe in an ECCE setting. This chapter expands on that topic and explores the role of hygiene. It is very important to observe the rules of hygiene and create a hygienic environment in the ECCE setting. Good hygiene prevents the spread of illnesses and infections (discussed in Chapters Two and Three) and helps to keep children safe in the ECCE setting. After reading this chapter you will be aware of hygiene risks in the ECCE setting and the steps that must be taken to deal with these risks.

INFECTION

Infection is caused when a germ or pathogen enters the body and multiplies, causing illness. There are two types of pathogens: bacteria and viruses. Chapter Three discussed some of the main viruses that pose a risk in the ECCE setting. Viruses and bacteria multiply quickly in the right conditions and are spread in three different ways:

1   direct contact
2   indirect contact
3   faeco-oral transmission.

Direct contact

Some infections are spread by direct contact with the pathogens that cause the infection. Direct contact can occur by touching (e.g. ringworm) or through breaks in the skin that allow pathogens to enter the bloodstream. This is known as **inoculation** and occurs when bacteria and viruses enter the body through cuts and grazes, providing a direct route of entry.

Indirect contact

Indirect contact occurs when the child encounters the pathogens indirectly, for example by inhalation or ingestion. **Inhalation** is when germs are spread by breathing in droplets in the air, for example from coughing and sneezing. Many colds, flus and other childhood viruses are spread in this way. **Ingestion** refers to swallowing bacteria and viruses. This can occur by ingesting contaminated food/drink or by putting toys or fingers into the mouth. Salmonella and E. coli are both spread by ingestion.

Faeco-oral transmission

Faeco-oral transmission occurs when germs are spread from the back passage to the mouth. This occurs when a child scratches or touches their bottom and then touches their mouth, thus **ingesting** the germs. Hand washing reduces the risk of faeco-oral transmission. Threadworms, gastroenteritis and diarrhoea are all spread by this method.

The chain of infection

Four steps are needed for infection to be spread, as illustrated in Figure 7.1.

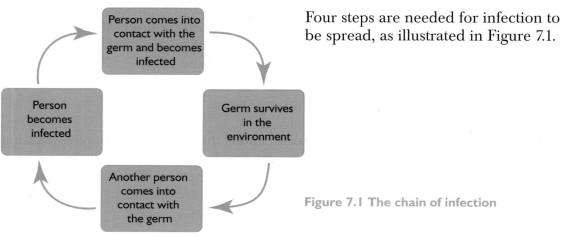

Figure 7.1 The chain of infection

Source: HSE 2012a

1 **A person comes into contact with the germ and becomes infected.** It is not always obvious if a child is carrying an illness. Some infected children will be asymptomatic, meaning they do not show any symptoms. Also, most illnesses have an incubation period during which the child is infectious but is not yet showing symptoms. Because of this it should be assumed that staff and children in the ECCE setting have an infection and safety procedures should be followed.

2 **The germ survives in the environment.** Bacteria and viruses are very hardy and can survive for some time in the environment. Even a small number of germs can be enough to cause illness, so hygiene measures are very important to kill any germs that enter the environment.

3 **Another person comes into contact with the germ.** A second person now comes into contact with the germ through one of the transmission methods described above (direct contact, indirect contact, faeco-oral transmission).

4 **This person becomes infected.** Adults with a well-developed and well-functioning immune system will be able to fight off most infections. However, children's immune systems are still developing and they are at a higher risk of developing an infection if they come into contact with pathogens. This risk is increased for young children in the ECCE setting.

PREVENTING INFECTION IN AN ECCE SETTING

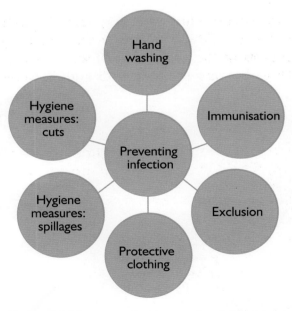

Figure 7.2 Measures for preventing infection

Hand washing

Every day our hands encounter thousands of germs when we touch contaminated surfaces or food, touch people and animals, and handle raw food. Washing hands with soap and running water will remove these germs and break the chain of infection. Hand washing is very important in an ECCE setting to prevent infection being spread. Staff must act as good role models for children and model the correct hand washing technique as recommended by the HSE and shown in Figure 7.3.

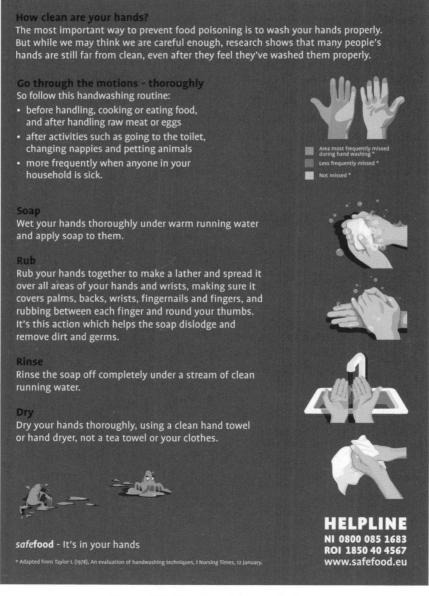

How clean are your hands?
The most important way to prevent food poisoning is to wash your hands properly. But while we may think we are careful enough, research shows that many people's hands are still far from clean, even after they feel they've washed them properly.

Go through the motions – thoroughly
So follow this handwashing routine:

- before handling, cooking or eating food, and after handling raw meat or eggs
- after activities such as going to the toilet, changing nappies and petting animals
- more frequently when anyone in your household is sick.

Area most frequently missed during hand washing *
Less frequently missed *
Not missed *

Soap
Wet your hands thoroughly under warm running water and apply soap to them.

Rub
Rub your hands together to make a lather and spread it over all areas of your hands and wrists, making sure it covers palms, backs, wrists, fingernails and fingers, and rubbing between each finger and round your thumbs. It's this action which helps the soap dislodge and remove dirt and germs.

Rinse
Rinse the soap off completely under a stream of clean running water.

Dry
Dry your hands thoroughly, using a clean hand towel or hand dryer, not a tea towel or your clothes.

*safe*food - It's in your hands

* Adapted from Taylor L (1978), An evaluation of handwashing techniques, I Nursing Times, 12 January.

HELPLINE
NI 0800 085 1683
ROI 1850 40 4567
www.safefood.eu

Figure 7.3 Hand washing technique

Tip

It can be difficult to get young children to lather their hands with soap for long enough to kill germs effectively. Teach children songs to sing while washing their hands to encourage them to scrub for long enough. For example:

Wash, wash, wash my hands
Make them nice and clean.
Rub the bottoms, and the tops
And fingers in between.
(Sung to the tune of 'Row, Row, Row Your Boat')

Or:

Twinkle, twinkle, little star
See how clean my two hands are.
Soap and water, wash and scrub,
Get those germs off, rub a dub.
Twinkle, twinkle, little star
See how clean my two hands are.
(Sung to the tune of 'Twinkle, Twinkle')

Standards of hand washing in an ECCE setting need to be higher than in a home setting because of the larger number of people in the setting. You must follow these guidelines.

- Keep your nails short and clean – germs can get trapped underneath longer nails. Nail extensions and false nails are not suitable for everyday wear in an ECCE setting. Similarly, rings will trap dirt, so they should not be worn, but a plain gold or silver band is allowed.
- Always use warm water and liquid soap when hand washing, and use a nail brush to remove dirt from under fingernails.
- Use paper towels to dry hands and throw away after use to prevent infection.
- Cover any cuts with a waterproof dressing to prevent cross-infection.
- Demonstrate to children how to wash their hands and supervise hand washing to ensure that they follow the correct procedure.
- As you will be washing your hands frequently, the skin on your hands may dry out. Prevent this by using a hand cream at home to keep skin in good condition.

ECCE staff should wash their hands:

▶ before starting a shift
▶ before eating, smoking, handling or preparing food or feeding a child
▶ before preparing meals, snacks and drinks
▶ after using the toilet or helping a child use the toilet
▶ after nappy changing
▶ after playing with or handling items in the playroom
▶ after dealing with bodily fluids – wiping runny noses, cleaning up vomit, etc.
▶ after handling waste
▶ after removing disposable gloves or aprons
▶ after handling pets or pet litter.

Children should be taught to wash their hands:

▶ after playing with pets
▶ after using the bathroom
▶ after sneezing, blowing their nose or coughing
▶ after touching an open cut or sore
▶ after playing outside
▶ before and after eating.

Hand washing products

Soap and anti-bacterial alcohol-based gels should be used for hand washing.

▶ **Soap** should be provided in all toilets in the setting and staff and children should be reminded to use it when hand washing. Liquid soap should be used as bar soap can be a source of contamination. The soap provided should be suitable for sensitive skin and anti-bacterial soap should be provided in the food preparation area.
▶ **Alcohol-based gels** are readily available over the counter in chemists and should have an alcohol content of 60% to be effective. Alcohol-based gels work best on hands that are not visibly dirty; hands should also be washed with soap. Children should be supervised when using alcohol gels so to ensure they do not ingest the gel.

Immunisation

Some diseases have such serious side effects that it is recommend that we immunise against them. Immunisation involves exposing the body to a treated form of the illness which will not make the person sick but will activate the body's defence system and make the person immune to further contact from the disease. The HSE has devised a schedule of recommended vaccinations for young children and it is recommended that all children are vaccinated. ECCE settings should keep records of what vaccinations children have. All staff members should be fully immunised.

Exclusion periods

When a child becomes ill they must be excluded from the setting until such time as they are no longer contagious. This is to prevent other children and staff becoming infected with the illness. Exclusion periods range from 48 hours to a week, depending on the illness. (There is a table outlining the exclusion periods for various common childhood illnesses in Appendix II.)

Wearing protective clothing

As an ECCE worker you will be involved in the physical care of children, wiping noses, nappy changing and toileting. When you are dealing with bodily fluids you must wear protective clothing. Gloves and aprons are usually used in an ECCE setting when dealing with bodily fluids such as urine, mucus and vomit. Wearing protective clothing helps to prevent the spread of infection and cross-infection through cuts and grazes.

Gloves and an apron should be worn when:

▶ changing nappies
▶ cleaning potties
▶ cleaning up blood or bodily fluids (e.g. vomit)
▶ cleaning in general
▶ handling waste.

Gloves and aprons should be disposable and thrown away after each use.

Cleaning up spillages of blood and bodily fluid

Any blood or bodily fluid spillages must be cleaned up immediately to prevent contamination. The HSE recommends the use of chlorine-based disinfectants to disinfect the area after a spillage of blood/bodily fluid.

Management of cuts

In the course of the rough and tumble of normal play, children will get cuts and bruises. Cuts and breaks in the skin must be covered to stop germs entering through the break in the skin. Absorbent materials should be used to stop the child bleeding and the cut covered with waterproof dressing. Gloves should be worn by staff members throughout.

FIRST AID KIT

Every ECCE setting must have a fully stocked first aid kit. Under the Child Care (Pre-school Services) (No. 2) Regulations 2006, a first aid kit for **children** must contain the following.

Table 7.1 Children's first aid kit

	1–5 children	6–25 children	26–50 children
Hypoallergenic plasters	12	20	20
Sterile eye pads (bandage attached)	2	6	6
Individually wrapped triangular bandages	2	6	6
Small individually wrapped sterile, unmedicated wound dressings	1	2	4
Medium individually wrapped non-stick, sterile, unmedicated wound dressings	1	2	4
Individually wrapped antiseptic wipes	8	8	10
Paramedic shears	1	1	1
Latex gloves – non-powdered latex or Nitril gloves (latex-free)	1 box	1 box	1 box
Sterile eye wash (where there is no running water)	1	2	2

In addition to a first aid box you could usefully have a fever scan thermometer and a pair of tough cut scissors.

MEDICINE CABINETS

Under the 2006 Regulations medicine cabinets must be placed out of reach of children and kept under lock and key. Medicines, sprays and lotions should **never** be stored in the first aid box and should be stored separately in the medicine cabinet. All medicines must be kept in their original containers and clearly labelled.

STERILISING BABIES' FEEDING EQUIPMENT

Feeding equipment for babies up to one year old must be sterilised. Sterilisation removes harmful bacteria that a baby's developing immune system cannot yet deal with. Before sterilising, wash all bottles, teats and covers in warm soapy water, using a bottle brush, to remove any milk residue. This should be done as soon after feeding as possible to prevent bacteria from multiplying. Three methods of sterilisation can be used.

1 **Steam sterilising** is a fast and efficient way of sterilising. The bottles, teats and caps are placed in the steam steriliser, following the manufacturer's instructions. Steam sterilising usually takes about ten minutes and is relatively hassle free.

Figure 7.4 Steam sterilising

2 **Cold water chemical sterilising** involves immersing the feeding equipment in a diluted disinfectant such as Milton. Chemical sterilisation usually takes about 15–30 minutes.

Figure 7.5 Chemical sterilising

3 **Boiling** is another method of sterilisation. Immerse the feeding equipment in a saucepan filled with cold water, cover the pan, bring to the boil and boil for at least three minutes.

Figure 7.6 Boiling

Note: Whichever method you use, you must be careful when removing the now sterile feeding equipment. Do not touch the equipment with your bare hands; use tongs to remove it. **Never** touch the teat of the bottle with your hands; use sterile tongs.

FOOD SAFETY AND HYGIENE

Food safety means protecting food from contamination by foreign objects, poison/chemicals and harmful bacteria (HSE 2012a). Food spoilage is caused by enzymes and micro-organisms and occurs when food is contaminated or prepared in a dirty kitchen or when the person handling the food is careless or unhygienic. Enzymes are the chemicals naturally present in fruit and vegetables, which cause food to ripen and then over-ripen. Micro-organisms include bacteria, yeasts and moulds. Food poisoning is caused when these micro-organisms get into food, which is then eaten. Bacteria carriers include: careless and unhygienic food handlers; a dirty food preparation area; dirty equipment, utensils and kitchen cloths; and flies, vermin and household pets in the kitchen.

Food poisoning

The most common bacteria that cause food poisoning in humans are:

▶ **Salmonella:** found in the intestines of humans, birds and animals.
▶ **Staphylococci:** found in the human body, nose, mouth, throat, cuts and boils.
▶ **Clostridium:** carried in the intestines of humans, birds and animals.

The symptoms of food poisoning are similar to those of viral gastroenteritis and include nausea, vomiting, diarrhoea, fever, and abdominal pain and cramps. Food poisoning can occur up to 36 hours after the ingestion of contaminated food.

Food poisoning is very serious but is entirely preventable by following basic food hygiene rules. Kitchen staff must clean and disinfect surfaces regularly to prevent bacteria flourishing. Equipment must be washed after use and stored in clean, dry presses. Kitchen cloths must be clean and kept separately from cloths used in other areas of the setting to prevent contamination. Animals should never be let into the kitchen and the kitchen should be kept free of flies. The kitchen should be bright, well ventilated and airy, the sink disinfected regularly and the floor swept and washed daily.

If the setting is operating a kitchen, all staff should receive **hazard analysis and critical control point (HACCP)** training. HACCP is a food safety management system that helps workers to identify biological, chemical and physical hazards and analyse the risk of how likely the hazard is to occur. After assessing the hazard and risk, the critical control point must be identified. This is the step in the food preparation process when the risk of the hazard occurring is high and must be controlled.

REST AND SLEEP IN THE ECCE SETTING

Sleep and rest are essential for health. During sleep, the cells of the body regenerate and are replenished, allowing healing to take place. Sleep is also essential for the brain to rest and to process what has happened during the day. Adults need approximately eight hours' sleep a night, but young children need much more sleep. A child in pre-school will need 12 hours' sleep, which can be made up with naps during the day in addition to sleep at night. Under the Pre-School Regulations (DoHC 2006), ECCE settings must provide facilities for rest and sleep. A sleep room must be available for children to nap during the day and rest areas should be made available for children who do not sleep during the day.

Sudden infant death syndrome (SIDS)

SIDS, sometimes known as cot death, is the sudden and unexplained death of an infant or young child. Despite many decades of research it is not clear what causes SIDS. However, research has identified factors that increase the risk of SIDS. The environment also has a role to play. Risk factors for SIDS include:

- the baby being put to sleep on their front
- the mother smoking during pregnancy or the baby being exposed to smoke after birth – the risk increases with every cigarette the mother smokes a day and with every smoker in the home
- overheating the baby by over-dressing or having too high a temperature in the room
- sharing a bed with a baby.

Preventing SIDS in the ECCE setting

A separate sleep room will be needed. The temperature must be tightly controlled, and kept between 16°C and 20°C. A thermometer must be available in the room and the temperature checked and recorded every hour. Babies must always be put **back to sleep** and **feet to foot**. In other words, they must be put to sleep on their backs, with their feet to the foot of the cot. This position is currently recommended as best practice in preventing SIDS. Cots should not contain pillows or duvets as these present a suffocation hazard. Babies should be checked regularly to make sure blankets do not slip over their head. When ECCE staff put children down to sleep, they should dress children as lightly as possible, in a nappy, vest and babygro. Bibs and ribbons present a strangulation hazard and should not be worn by children when asleep or upset. Tummy time, when the baby spends time on their stomach, should be encouraged to strengthen the muscles in the baby's stomach, shoulders and neck.

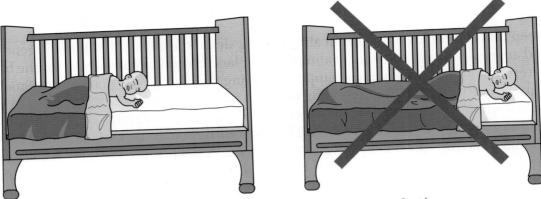

Figure 7.7 Put babies 'back to sleep' and 'feet to foot'

Preventing SIDS at home

The same guidelines for preventing SIDS in the ECCE setting apply at home. Babies should be put to sleep in a cot in their parents' room and the cot should remain in the parents' room for at least the first six months. Sharing a bed with the child is discouraged as the baby can become overheated. In particular, the baby should never sleep in the parents' bed if:

- either parent smokes
- either parent has been drinking or has taken drugs or medication that may make them sleep more heavily
- either parent is extremely tired
- the baby is less than three months old
- the baby was born prematurely (before 37 weeks)
- the baby weighed less than 2.5kg (5.5lb) at birth.

Parents must never fall asleep with a baby in their arms on an armchair, couch or beanbag. Some research shows that giving a child a soother every time they are placed to sleep reduces the risk of cot death, but the use of a soother will be down to the parents' personal choice.

POLICIES AND PROCEDURES IN ECCE SETTINGS

In order to meet Standard Nine of Síolta – Health and Welfare – the setting must devise and implement a range of policies and procedures (CECDE 2006). Component 9.1 states that:

> The setting has implemented a full range of policies and procedures to prevent the spread of infectious diseases, reduce exposure to environmental hazards and stress, and deal effectively and efficiently with medical situations that may arise.

This is supported by component 9.2:

> The setting endeavours, through the implementation of a range of policies, procedures and actions, to promote the health of all children and adults.

Síolta requires that settings implement a range of policies and procedures covering the following categories:

- overarching statements
- health and safety
- child welfare
- curriculum
- partnership with families and liaison
- human resources
- administration.

What are policies and procedures?
A *policy* is a statement of principles, values or intent that guides or usually determines decisions and actions to achieve an organisation's goals. . . . *Procedures* spell out precisely what action is to be taken in line with the relevant policy and outline the steps to be followed or the way a task is to be performed. (Willoughby 2008:21)

Essentially, policies comprise the **rules** of the setting (e.g. promoting healthy eating) and a procedure outlines how exactly the policy is to be **implemented** (e.g. a ban on unhealthy food, regular healthy eating week).

Drawing up policies and procedures

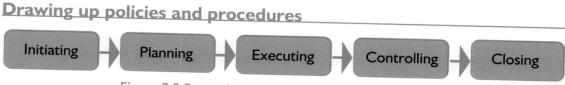

Figure 7.8 Stages in developing policies and procedures

1 **Initiate the process:** Set up a working group; choose which polices are to be drawn up.

2 **Plan:** Begin to plan the policy; gather the information necessary – best practice, legal requirements – to write a comprehensive policy.

3 **Execute:** Devise the policy.

4 **Control:** Check the policy to ensure that it reflects the views of the working group; make adjustments; decide whether to accept the document.

5 **Close:** The working group signs off the document and the policy/procedure is put into practice; a review date is set.

When writing your policies and procedures, ensure that they are:

▶ **Inclusive:** Involving every member of the setting and all diverse groups in the setting.

▶ **Realistic:** Easily put into practice in the 'real world'.

▶ **Fair:** The policy and procedure should explain why they are needed and how they will improve the setting.

▶ **Consultative:** Everybody should be included in the process – staff, parents and children.

▶ **Applicable:** Policies and procedures should be a good fit for the setting and easy to put into practice.

▶ **Reviewed:** All procedures should be reviewed regularly to keep up to date with best practice and legislative requirements.

▶ **Distributed:** Policies and procedures are designed to be used. They should therefore be distributed to each member of staff and parents so that they can be implemented (McPartland 2012).

The Child Health and Well-being module requires you to be familiar with the following polices:

▶ security

▶ fire evacuation

▶ first aid

▶ accident and incident

▶ illness

▶ exclusion

▶ notifiable illnesses

▶ healthy eating.

Signpost for reflection

ECCE settings are required to have many policies and procedures to promote a safe and healthy environment. How can staff, parents and children work together to ensure that all of these are implemented?

Table 7.2 Policies in an ECCE setting

Policy	What the policy should include
Security policy	Measures taken to secure the setting, including use of CCTV, access systems and passwords Garda vetting procedure
Fire evacuation policy	Evacuation procedure and evacuation routes How often the evacuation procedure is to be practised Name of designated fire officer
First aid policy	Definition of 'first aid' List of trained first aiders Contents of first aid kit Procedure for keeping first aid qualifications up to date Legal requirements
Accident/incident policy	Definition of 'accident' and 'incident' List of legal obligations Procedure to be followed in the event of an accident/incident, including completion of accident books
Illness policy	Definition of 'illness' Procedure to be followed if a child becomes ill while in the pre-school, including the provision of a quiet room Procedures to prevent illness, including staff hygiene, children's hygiene, cleaning routines and kitchen hygiene
Exclusion policy	Definition of 'exclusion'; circumstances under which exclusion is necessary Exclusion periods for staff and children for a range of illnesses as per HSE guidelines
Notifiable illnesses policy	Definition of 'notifiable illness' List of notifiable illnesses Procedure for informing the HSE of a notifiable illness
Healthy eating policy	Definition of 'healthy eating' How the setting promotes healthy eating, e.g. healthy eating week Examples of healthy lunches and a list of 'banned' food

chapter eight

Applying Developmental Knowledge to Promote Child Health and Well-being

LEARNING OUTCOMES

After reading this chapter you will be able to:

▶ discuss the importance of physical development
▶ plan activities to promote children's physical well-being
▶ show an understanding of how secure and positive relationship with adults and children are formed, with particular reference to Bowlby, Ainsworth, Rutter and Schafer
▶ explain Gibbs' reflective cycle and use it in your own practice.

PHYSICAL DEVELOPMENT

The ability to develop physical skills depends on both the child's maturation and the provision of appropriate experiences. The child needs to be developmentally ready in order to develop physically – for example, no six-month-old will be ready to walk. They also need to be provided with appropriate developmental experiences and given opportunities to run, walk, crawl and practise their emerging physical strength. This is known as the interaction of nature and nurture and will be discussed in more detail in your Child Development module.

Physical development is a key part of the pre-school curriculum and must be incorporated into the pre-school's routine and curriculum plan. Aim 2 of the theme of Well-being in Aistear is that 'Children will be as healthy and fit as can be'. This is broken down into six learning goals. Children should:

1 gain increasing control and co-ordination of body movements
2 be aware of their bodies, their bodily functions, and their changing abilities
3 discover, explore and refine gross and fine motor skills

4   use self-help skills in caring for their own bodies

5   show good judgement when taking risks

6   make healthy choices and demonstrate positive attitudes to nutrition, hygiene, exercise and routine.

Physical development is important in all areas of children's well-being. Physical competence makes new behaviours possible and determines potential experiences in everyday life. As children become physically stronger they are better able to explore their environment, for example becoming able to pull themselves to a standing position to look out of a window. As the child becomes more confident and competent in their physical skills they become able to engage in co-operative play, thus developing social skills. Physical development is needed for schooling – children need to be able to hold a pencil in order to learn to write. Physical competence also affects children's self-esteem. As children grow and develop they become more physically capable and this increases their sense of mastery and self-esteem.

In order for children to develop physical skills, an appropriate curriculum incorporating opportunities for them to exercise and engage in physical activity is needed. As we discussed in Chapter Five, young children need to get one hour of physical activity per day. This can be achieved by providing opportunities for the physical activities shown in Figure 8.1.

Figure 8.1 Physical activities in the ECCE setting

THINK ABOUT IT

How can we provide opportunities to engage in different physical activities in pre-school?

Physical development and emotional well-being

The phrase 'healthy body, healthy mind' illustrates the link between physical and emotional well-being. Researchers now know that our physical and emotional development are strongly linked. Physical exercise has the following benefits for emotional well-being.

- It helps to promote a positive attitude.
- It helps to release inner aggression and negative feelings.
- As children develop physically they gain in confidence and independence (emotional development).
- As children develop physically and engage in physical exercise they feel in control and powerful.

EMOTIONAL WELL-BEING

Aim One of Aistear's theme of Well-being states that children will be strong psychologically and socially. This is broken down into six learning goals:

1 make strong attachments and develop warm and supportive relationships with family peers and adults in out-of-home settings and in their community
2 be aware of and name their own feelings, and understand that others may have different feelings
3 handle transitions and changes well
4 be confident and self-reliant
5 respect themselves, others and the environment
6 make decisions and choices about their own learning and development.

THINK ABOUT IT

How can we promote the emotional well-being of children in an ECCE setting?

ATTACHMENT THEORY

As you will learn in your Child Development class, emotional development is an essential aspect of children's development. This includes the development of emotional security and forming bonds of attachment with others. An attachment is a 'close emotional relationship between two people' (Shaffer 2005:131). Child development theorists emphasis the importance of attachment for babies and young children.

In the past it was believed that babies and young children could only form a bond of attachment with one person, usually the mother. **John Bowlby**, one of the first major attachment theorists, worked in a home for abandoned boys and developed a theory of **maternal deprivation**. Bowlby believed that if children were separated from their mother in early life they would develop emotional problems in later life. Bowlby's theory is controversial as it implies that only the mother – not other family members – can be an attachment figure for the child.

Mary Ainsworth worked with Bowlby and was interested in measuring types of attachment. She designed an experiment known as the 'strange situation', which can be performed with children aged 12–18 months. In the experiment, the baby is separated from mother and their reaction is observed. Three types of attachment were found, and a fourth was later added by Main and Solomon (1990):

1 secure
2 insecure: detached/avoidant
3 insecure: resistant/ambivalent
4 disorganised.

In **secure attachment** the baby readily separates from the caregiver and prefers the mother to a stranger. The baby greets the mother with pleasure when they are reunited and is easily reassured. Secure attachment is shown by up to 65% of babies.

There are two sub-types of **insecure attachment**: detached/avoidant; and resistant/ambivalent attachment.

In **detached/avoidant** attachment the baby avoids contact with the mother, especially at reunion. The baby does not resist contact but makes little effort and shows no preference for the mother over a stranger. Detached/avoidant attachment is displayed by up to 20% of babies.

In **resistant/ambivalent** attachment the baby shows little exploration of their environment and is wary of strangers. The baby becomes upset at reunion and is not reassured by the mother's return. Resistant/ambivalent attachment is evident in up to 15% of babies.

In **disorganised** attachment babies appear dazed, confused and fearful, showing patterns of both avoidant and resistant attachment. Only 5% of babies show disorganised attachment.

Attachment styles: do they matter?

It is important to note that there is no 'right' style of attachment. Evidence suggests that some attachment styles are more prevalent in some cultures than others, suggesting a role for cultural differences. For example, higher rates of avoidant attachment are found in German babies and higher rates of resistant attachment in Japanese babies. What is important is the 'fit' between the child and parent or carer. This means that the way a parent or carer responds to a child can be more important than the child's underlying attachment style.

Multiple attachments

As discussed above, the work of Bowlby and Ainsworth is based on the assumption that babies attach to one person, usually the mother. This theory of **monotropism** has been criticised for excluding and ignoring the emotional bond that exists between children and their father, grandparents and other adults. Research now indicates that babies and young children can and do make multiple attachments, and attach to more than one person (Schaffer & Emerson 1964; Rutter 1981). This is true even for very young babies. In 1964 two researchers, Rudolph Schaffer and Peggy Emerson, designed a study to investigate attachments in babies. The results showed that babies experienced multiple attachments and could have distinct bonds of attachment with several people.

At seven months:

▶ 29% of the babies had developed a bond of attachment with **more than one** person.
▶ 10% of the babies had developed a bond of attachment with **five or more** people.

At ten months:

▶ 59% of babies had developed a bond of attachment with **more than one** person.

At 18 months:

▶ 87% of babies had developed a bond of attachment with **more than one** person.

Research indicates that children can and do form attachments with many key people in their lives, including father, grandparents, aunts and uncles, brothers and sisters and childcare workers. Even very small babies have distinct relationships with different people, and the child attaching to many people is a factor in emotional well-being. In the words of Rudolph Schaffer, 'love has no limits' (1977:100).

Attachment in childcare

As you might imagine, a great deal of research has focused on attachment in childcare. Michael Rutter is an eminent developmental psychologist who has written extensively about attachments in childcare settings. Rutter argues that if the care provided is stable and of good quality there will be no detrimental effect on children, and this has led to the introduction of the **key person** approach in settings. The key person is someone specially assigned to a number of children who develops a particular relationship with the individual children for whom they are a key person. This helps children to settle in at the setting and lessens any separation anxiety they may feel when leaving their carer.

The role of the adult is essential for providing for children's emotional well-being in ECCE. The Effective Provision of Pre-school Education (EPPE) project found that children make most progress when cared for by warm staff who respond to their needs. This is also highlighted in Aistear, which emphasises the need for a 'reciprocal relationship' between the child and carer.

QUALITY ECCE SETTINGS: FOCUS ON THE ECCE WORKER

Quality ECCE workers are needed for a quality ECCE setting. **Reflective practice** is a useful method of thinking about your practice as an ECCE worker. Using reflective practice you can identify your strengths and weaknesses and find ways to make improvements. Gibbs' reflective cycle is a method of reflective practice which you may find useful both during your studies and in your professional career.

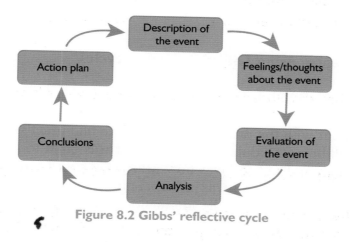

Figure 8.2 Gibbs' reflective cycle

▶ **Description:** Describe factually what happened. Tell the story of the event and include as much information as you can.

▶ **Feelings:** Identify and discuss how you felt during the event. Discuss how you felt when you began the task, during the task and on completing the task. Be careful not to just state how you felt – explain **why** you felt this way. It's not enough to say 'I felt nervous' – explain why you felt this way.

▶ **Evaluation:** Having described the event and your feelings, it's time to make an evaluation. Overall, was it a good or bad experience? Why was it a good/bad experience? Again, remember to **explain** your points.

▶ **Analysis:** In the analysis stage, you attempt to make sense of what has happened. Ask yourself questions about what happened at each stage, and compare what should have happened with what actually happened.

▶ **Conclusion:** Draw a conclusion based on the event. What did you learn? What would you do differently next time?

▶ **Action plan:** Having described what you would change, you must now make an action plan for the future. Building on the experience, what will you do next time? What changes will you have to make and how will you make them? Set yourself a goal for the next day of placement based on today's events.

> EXERCISE

> Describe a day on placement using Gibbs' reflective cycle. You may be able to use this as a diary entry for your Early Education Care and Practice module.

Sample diary entry using Gibbs' reflective cycle

Description of event: Today on placement I was asked to help with the nappy-changing routine. Mary the supervisor got me to observe her changing nappies first. I was familiar with the procedure because we had practised it in our Child Health and Well-being module in college but it was great to see it with a 'real live' baby! One thing I noticed was how Mary spoke and sang to the babies as she changed their nappies. This was just what our teacher had told us and I could see the children really enjoyed the interaction. Mary then showed me how to fill in the record books. More paperwork! After I had watched her, Mary said it was my turn. I gathered my equipment together, washed my hands and picked up George. I followed the procedure as I had been shown in college. Mary was there to support and encourage me – and to remind me if I made mistakes!

When I undid George's nappy I got a shock when I was sprayed! Mary laughed and said 'these things happen with boys'. I will know to watch out for that next time. After finishing with George I filled in the record book. I changed three more nappies that day and am glad I got the chance to practise the skill.

Feelings: When Mary said it was time for me to change nappies I felt really nervous. I had never changed a real baby's nappy before and had only practised using dolls in college. I knew that I knew what to do, but I also knew that changing a real baby's nappy would be very different from changing a doll's nappy. I was worried in case they would wriggle out of my arms or twist and turn while I was trying to change them. But I knew this was a really important skill to learn so I took a deep breath and got stuck in! I was quite proud that Mary had asked me to help because I knew she wouldn't have done so if she didn't think I was capable. It made me feel really like part of the team and a 'real staff member'. When I was changing George's nappy I felt really nervous. I was worried I would do something wrong. When he sprayed me I got such a shock! I was a bit embarrassed but I soon saw the funny side. Looking back now I fell really glad that I did the nappy changing today. I'm proud of myself and I feel a lot more confident in my nappy-changing skills.

Evaluation: Changing nappies was a mixed experience. It was a good experience because I completed the task. This has helped me to be more confident in my skills. However, I think my nerves were a drawback and this is something I have to work on. I also got sprayed when I removed George's nappy. Next time I will remember to be careful when changing boys' nappies.

Analysis: Because I was nervous I was hesitant when Mary asked me to change the nappies. This is something I need to work on. I should be eager for new learning experiences in the crèche. Next time I will try to volunteer for new tasks and not be so nervous. I should also have remembered that boys can spray when their nappy is taken off. Next time I will be prepared for this.

Conclusion: I think I learned a lot today. I learned not to be so nervous when asked to do new tasks. I got to practise a valuable skill and I have grown in confidence as a result.

Action plan: Having completed nappy changing today I intend to practise this skill further on other work placement days. Today went really well, but practice makes perfect and if I want to work in childcare I will have to be completely competent at changing nappies. I also need to remember that boys have a tendency to spray when the nappy is opened. I got caught out today, but I will be prepared in future! Finally, I want to try to practise new skills on placement. Now that I have tried nappy changing I am going to ask if I can try different tasks. So far I haven't spoonfed or bottlefed the babies. Over the next few weeks I will set myself the challenge of completing both these tasks, and really practising my practical skills.

Signpost for reflection

Reflect on the daily routine and curriculum of your work experience setting. How does the setting provide for children's physical and emotional well-being? Are there areas that could do with improvement? How could either the routine or the curriculum be improved in order to promote children's physical and emotional well-being?

Section Four

APPENDICES

Sample Letter Informing Parents of the Outbreak of an Infectious Disease in the Setting

Dear Parent or Guardian,

There has been a case of chickenpox in your child's crèche/pre-school and your child may have been exposed. If your child has not had chickenpox before it is quite likely that he/she will catch it.

What is chickenpox?

Chickenpox is a common childhood illness. Fever and cold symptoms are often the first signs of illness and are followed by the appearance of the typical rash. The rash starts as small pink bumps, often around the neck, ears, back and stomach. These develop a little water blister, which in turn becomes yellow and oozy and ultimately crusty as it dries. The rash spreads outwards to the whole body, finally involving the lower arms and legs. People may have only a few spots or may be virtually covered with them. In children it is usually a relatively mild illness; however, occasionally complications develop.

Why should I be concerned about chickenpox?

Chickenpox can be a devastating infection in people with a seriously weakened immune system (e.g. patients with leukaemia or following an organ transplantation). In adults, chickenpox is a much more significant illness than in children and there is a greater risk of complications developing. Chickenpox in pregnancy can cause severe illness and, if contracted in the early stages of pregnancy, may result in abnormalities in the baby.

What should I do now?

If your child is normally healthy, chickenpox is likely to be a relatively mild illness and no specific precautions are necessary. Symptoms usually develop 10 to 21 days after exposure. The infected person can spread infection for up to three days before the rash appears and until the last pox is crusted and dry. If your child has a weakened immune system, please contact your doctor and let them know that they may have been exposed.

What should I do if I think my child has chickenpox?

If you suspect chickenpox, do not bring the child into a crowded surgery waiting room, as this may only spread the infection further. Contact your doctor to confirm the diagnosis. Do not use aspirin or any products that contain aspirin to control fever if your child has chickenpox, as this has been associated with the development of a rare but serious disease called Reye's syndrome.

Can my child stay in crèche/pre-school?

Many children with chickenpox are too sick to attend pre-school and are more comfortable at home. Children can spread the infection to others as long as they still have any spots that are not crusted and dried. Children with chickenpox or shingles should be excluded from pre-school until scabs are dry. This is usually five to seven days after the appearance of the rash. Children with spots that are crusted and dried can safely attend school.

Thank you for giving this your attention. Your family doctor will be able to answer any further questions that you might have about chickenpox.

Yours sincerely,

(HSE 2012a)

appendix II
Exclusion Periods for ECCE Settings

Illness	Exclusion period
Chickenpox	5–7 days after the rash disappears
Conjunctivitis	Exclusion not always necessary
Diarrhoea	48 hours from last episode
Gastroenteritis	48 hours since last episode of vomiting/diarrhoea
Hand, foot and mouth disease	Until the blisters disappear from the child's hands
Impetigo	Until lesions are healed or crusted or 24 hours after starting antibiotics
Influenza	7 days
Measles	5 days after the rash appears
Meningitis	Child will be too ill to attend setting
Mumps	5 days after swelling begins
Rubella	7 days after the rash appears
Scarlet fever	Child can return once they have taken antibiotics for 24 hours
Tuberculosis	Until no longer infectious
Vomiting	48 hours from last vomiting episode

appendix III

Child Health and Well-being Module: Assessment

There are two areas of assessment in the Child Health and Well-being module:

- skills demonstration: 60%
- project: 40%.

SKILLS DEMONSTRATION

This is designed to test your ability to carry out personal care routines. You are required to carry out a sample of the following tasks.

- Cleaning and sterilising a baby's bottle.
- Preparing a formula bottle feed.
- Topping and tailing a baby.
- Changing a baby's nappy.
- Bathing a baby.
- Spoon feeding.
- Taking a temperature.

Most colleges will require these tasks to be carried out in a simulated environment using dolls instead of real babies. Many students are nervous when doing the skills demonstration – don't be! Your tutor will have given you lots of time to practise in the classes before the test, so make sure to use this time well. Remember: practice makes perfect!

You are also required to:

- keep records of the task
- show application of knowledge.

You will be marked under the following criteria.

Effective Implementation of Task (20%)

This is marked under three sub-headings:

1 Organisation and Preparation
2 Communication
3 Health and Safety.

Organisation and Preparation

You will score highly here if you are well prepared for the task. Gather all the equipment you need in one place before you begin the task – this shows that you are well prepared and organised.

Communication

Communication and interaction are really important when working with young children. During your skills demonstration you must show the examiner how you will communicate and interact with babies in the 'real world'. Sing, chat and talk to the baby just as you would in real life. Use a soft tone of voice, just as you would with a real baby. Sometimes students are nervous or embarrassed about doing this. Don't be – your tutor has seen it all before! If you do not talk and sing to the doll during the demonstrations you **will** lose the marks allocated for communication.

Health and Safety

Marks are allocated for holding the baby in a safe and secure manner, paying particular attention to the head. Make sure to wash your hands before and after the task and wear protective equipment. You will lose marks in this section if:

- you leave the baby unattended at any stage in the task
- you do not check the temperature of the water when bathing the baby
- you touch the teat of a sterilised bottle.

Accurate Record of Task (10%)

At the end of the Skills Demonstration you are required to complete a short exercise describing exactly what you did in both tasks. This will usually involve writing a step-by-step account of each task.

Extensive Range of Practical Skills Displayed Competently (10%)

Ten marks are available here for completing both tasks accurately and effectively. You will lose marks here if you complete the task in an incorrect sequence or if you forget a step in the task.

Insightful Reflective Journal (10%)

In this section you may be asked to complete a reflective journal based on your learning in the Child, Health and Well-being module. Alternatively, they may ask you reflective questions during the practical exam. Gibbs' reflective cycle may be used as an aid in the writing process. Your tutor will guide you on the format of this journal, but you may choose to base the journal on experiences from a work placement or use the 'Signposts for reflection' at the end of each chapter of this book as a springboard for the reflective process.

Good Application of Knowledge (10%)

Marks are allocated in this section for the extent of your knowledge of child health and well-being. In the practical exam, your tutor may test this by asking questions. Questions might include:

- Name two main causes of nappy rash.
- What temperature should a baby's bath be?

PROJECT

The project is worth 40% of the total module marks. You are required to discuss in detail the health and safety requirements for children in an ECCE setting. These include:

- health and safety regulations
- the factors that contribute to the overall well-being of children
- the components of a balanced diet, including a menu for one day
- indoor and outdoor safety
- signs and symptoms of the unwell child.

The project *could* take the following format.

Introduction

▷ Introduce the type of setting you are writing about and the age group of the children.

▷ Explain what needs children have in a childcare setting. You could refer to developmental needs (PILES) or Maslow's hierarchy of human needs (Chapter Four).

Legislative requirements

Provide an overview of the legislation governing an ECCE setting. Remember to focus on the requirements of the Pre-school Services Regulations 2006 and the Safety, Health and Welfare at Work Act 2005. You could also refer to your obligations under Síolta and Aistear. (*Hint:* re-read Chapter One of this book before writing this section.)

Children's well-being

This section focuses on how the ECCE worker promotes children's health and well-being in pre-school. Explain the routes of infection and how they relate to a pre-school setting, and discuss the factors affecting children's health. You could conclude by outlining the signs and symptoms of illness in children.

Indoor and outdoor safety

Here you must discuss how to promote indoor and outdoor safety. You could start with a risk assessment of the setting. Outline and explain what potential hazards there are in the outdoor area and inside the setting. Then explain how these hazards could be dealt with or avoided, giving examples of safety equipment. Make sure to focus on how the childcare worker can promote indoor and outdoor safety. (*Hint:* re-read Chapter Six of this book before writing this section.)

Nutrition

Here you must show your knowledge of child nutrition. Begin by explaining what is meant by a balanced diet, using the food pyramid as a guide. Then give a short outline of the sources and uses of the three main nutrients – carbohydrates, lipids and protein – and some key minerals and vitamins. Having discussed children's basic nutrition requirements, outline and explain the *Food and Nutrition Guidelines for Pre-School Services* (DoHC 2004). Conclude by outlining a suitable menu for a pre-school for one day. Explain how the menu will meet children's nutritional needs. (*Hint:* re-read Chapter Five of this book before writing this section.)

Health

You could then outline the signs and symptoms of some common childhood illnesses. Include the vaccination schedule and explain why it is important to vaccinate.

Evaluation/conclusions/recommendations

Discuss what you have learned from the project. How will you promote children's health and well-being? Make recommendations you would suggest to promote children's health, hygiene, nutrition and safety in pre-school. For example:

- activities to promote healthy eating/personal care routines
- updated cleaning routines
- updated safety routines.

Tip

When you are writing your project, be sure to **SEE** when you are making a point:

- **S**tate your point.
- **E**xplain what you mean.
- Give an **E**xample.

For example:

Carbohydrates are the body's preferred energy source. This means that the human body needs carbohydrates in order to keep going. It is recommended that adults eat six servings of carbohydrates every day. An example of a serving would be one slice of wholemeal bread or half a cup of cooked rice or pasta.

Marking criteria

Good structure with introduction and bibliography (5%).

- Is the project well structured, with a beginning, middle and end?
- Is there a comprehensive introduction?
- Is there a comprehensive bibliography, using correct referencing style?
- Are all sources referenced appropriately throughout the project?

Clear understanding of the role and responsibilities of the childcare worker (5%).

▸ Does the candidate show an understanding of the role of the childcare worker in promoting children's health and safety?
▸ Are issues explored and related to ECCE settings?
▸ Are the responsibilities of the childcare worker made clear throughout the project?

Comprehensive exploration of health and safety issues in childcare, supported by current legislation (10%). Are the following areas explored in detail?

▸ Legislative requirements, including the Pre-school Regulations and their implications for the health and safety of young children.
▸ Nutritional requirements for children in pre-school, to include a description of the food pyramid, main nutrients needed by children, *Food and Nutrition Guidelines for Pre-School Services* (DoHC 2004). Is a sample menu for one day included?

Detailed description of well-being factors (10%):

▸ Are children's health issues explored?
▸ Is there an overview of child health promotion?
▸ Does the candidate show an understanding of common childhood illnesses?

Clear evaluation, conclusion and recommendations (10%).

▸ Are comprehensive recommendations made to promote children's health and safety in ECCE settings?

Please note: these points are for guidance only: each tutor will devise their own marking scheme.

Bibliography

Ainsworth, M. (1979) 'Infant–mother attachment', *American Psychologist*, 34, 932–7.

Asthma Society of Ireland (website) 'Asthma in Ireland' <http://asthmasociety.ie/asthma-information/asthma-in-ireland> accessed 20 July 2012.

Bowlby, J. (1969) *Attachment and Loss* (Vol. 1). London: Hogarth Press.

Brainwave: the Irish Epilepsy Association (website) 'Epilepsy: Did you Know That?' <www.epilepsy.ie/assets/41/4541B5F9-D04F-0008-96816519C28C690C_document/Did_You_Know.pdf> accessed 15 August 2012.

Brooks, A.-M., Hanafin, S., Cahill, H., Nic Gabhainn, S. and Molcho, M. (2010). *State of the Nation's Children 2010*. Dublin: DoHC.

Casey, M. and Phelan, A. (2008) 'Introducing Bug Busting: An Action Research to Treat and Prevent Head Lice' <www.ichn.ie/uploads/Bug_Busting_An_Action_Research_Study_to_Treat_and_Prevent_Head_Lice.pdf> accessed 14 July 2012.

Centre for Early Childhood Development and Education (CECDE) (2006) *Síolta: the National Quality Framework for Early Childhood Education*. Dublin: CECDE.

Childcare Act 1991 (1991). Dublin: Stationery Office.

Coleman, D. (2007) *Parenting is Child's Play: How to Give Your Child the Best Start in Life and Have Fun Doing It*. Dublin: Penguin Ireland.

Department of Children and Youth Affairs (2011) *Children First: National Guidelines for the Protection and Welfare of Children* (revised). Dublin: Department of Children and Youth Affairs.

Department of Health (2012) 'Your Guide to Healthy Eating Using the Food Pyramid' <www.dohc.ie/publications/pdf/YourGuide_HealthyEating_FoodPyramid.pdf?direct=1> accessed 1 July 2012.

Department of Health and Children (DoHC) (1999) *Children First: National Guidelines for the Protection and Welfare of Children*. Dublin: DoHC.

– (2000) *National Children's Strategy*. Dublin: DoHC.

– (2002) *Our Duty to Care*. Dublin: DoHC.

– (2004) *Food and Nutrition Guidelines for Pre-School Services*. Dublin: Health Promotion Unit, DoHC.

– (2005) *Breastfeeding in Ireland: A Five-Year Strategic Action Plan*. Dublin: DoHC.

– (2006) *Child Care (Pre-school Services) (No. 2) Regulations*. Dublin: Stationery Office.

Disability Act 2005 (2005). Dublin: Stationery Office.

Donohoe, J. and Gaynor, F. (2011). *Education and Care in the Early Years* (4th edn). Dublin: Gill & Macmillan.

Dunne, T., Farrell, P. and Kelly, V. (2009) *Feed Your Child Well* (3rd edn). Dublin: A. A. Farmar.

Economic and Social Research Institute (ESRI) and Trinity College Dublin (TCD) (various dates). *Growing Up in Ireland: National Longitudinal Study of Children.* Dublin: Department of Children and Youth Affairs: www.growingup.ie.

Flood, E. (2010a) *Assisting Children with Special Needs.* Dublin: Gill & Macmillan.

– (2010b) *Child Development for Students in Ireland.* Dublin: Gill & Macmillan.

Health Promotion Unit (HPU) (2006) *Infection in School: A Guide for School Personnel.* Dublin: HPU.

Health and Safety Authority (HSA) (2010) *Code of Practice on Preventing Accidents to Children and Young Persons in Agriculture* <www.hsa.ie/eng/Publications_and_ Forms_of_Practice/The_Children_and_Young_Persons_in_Agriculture_COP_. pdf> accessed 15 August 2012.

Health Service Executive (HSE) (2006) *Starting to Spoonfeed Your Baby.* Dublin: HSE.

– (2012a) *Management of Infectious Diseases in Childcare Facilities and Other Childcare Settings.* Dublin: HSE.

– (2012b) 'Urinary Tract Infection in Children' <www.hse.ie/eng/services/flu/A-Z/U/Urinary-tract-infection,-children/Intro.html> accessed 20 August 2012.

– (website) 'Benefits of Breastfeeding' <www.breastfeeding.ie> accessed 5 July 2012.

Irish Independent (2010) 'Coping with bedwetting', 7 May <www.independent.ie/ lifestyle/parenting/coping-with-bedwetting-2170727.html> accessed 24 July 2012.

Irish Nutrition and Dietetic Institute (2010) 'Food Allergies and Intolerance' <www. indi.ie/docs/1288_foodallergyfactsheet.pdf> accessed 30 July 2012.

Irish Times (2012) 'Child safety guidelines warn about window blinds' <www. irishtimes.com/newspaper/ireland/2012/0817/1224322324691.html> accessed 20 August 2012.

Irish Water Safety (website) <www.iws.ie> accessed 15 July 2012.

Kelly, C., Gavin, A., Molcho, M. and Nic Gabhainn, S. (2012) *The Irish Health Behaviours in School-aged Children (HBSC) Study 2010.* Dublin: Department of Health.

Layte, R. and McCroy, C. (2008) *Overweight and Obesity among Nine-year-olds.* Dublin: Office of the Minister for Children.

Main, M. and Solomon, J. (1990) 'Procedures for Identifying Infants as Disorganised/ Disorientated during the Ainsworth Strange Situation' in M.T. Greenberg, D. Cicchetti and E.M. Cummings (eds) *Attachment in the Preschool Years: Theory, Research and Intervention*, pp. 121–160. Chicago: University of Chicago Press.

Maslow, A. (1954) *Personality and Motivation.* New York: Harper & Row.

McPartland, E. (2010) *The Best Interests of the Child.* Dublin: Gill & Macmillan.

– (2012) *Supervision and Leadership in Childcare.* Dublin: Gill & Macmillan.

National Consumer Agency (nd) *A Guide to Toy Safety.* Dublin: NCA www.nsai.ie/ NSAI/files/8d/8d1f4cdf-4b0b-4b73-bb15-e74a56c34259.pdf.

National Council for Curriculum and Assesment (NCCA) (2009) *Aistear: the Early Childhood Curriculum Framework.* Dublin: NCCA.

National Immunisation Office (2011) *Your Child's Immunisation: A Guide for Parents.* Dublin: National Immunisation Office.

Office of the Minster for Children (2006) *Diversity and Equality Guidelines for Childcare Providers.* Dublin: Office of the Minister for Children.

Picoult, J. (2004) *My Sister's Keeper.* Sevenoaks, Kent: Hodder & Stoughton.

Rutter, M (1981) *Maternal Deprivation Reassessed* (2nd edn). Harmondsworth: Penguin.

Safety, Health and Welfare at Work Act 2005 (2005). Dublin: Stationery Office.

Schaffer, H.R. (1977) *Mothering.* Cambridge, MA: Harvard University Press.

Schaffer, H.R. and Emerson, P.E. (1964) 'The development of social attachments in infancy', *Monographs of the Society for Research in Child Development* 29, 94.

Shaffer, D.R. (2005) *Social and Personality Development* (5th edn). London: Thomson Learning.

Stoppard, M. (2006) *Child Health.* London: Dorling Kindersley.

Tipperary North County Council (website) 'Eco Nappies' <www.tipperarynorth.ie/environment/env_edu_awa.html > accessed 20 June 2012

United Nations Treaty Collection (1989) *United Nations Convention on the Rights of the Child.*

Walton, J. (2012) *National Pre-School Nutrition Survey: Summary Report on Food and Nutrient Intakes, Physical Measurements and Barriers to Healthy Eating* <www.iuna.net/wp-content/uploads/2012/06/Summary_Report_National_PreSchool_Nutrition_Survey_June_2012.pdf> accessed 30 June 2012.

Williams, J. and Greene, S. (2010) *Infants and their Families.* Dublin: Office of the Minster for Children.

Willoughby, M. (2008) *A Practical Guide to Developing Childcare Policies.* Dublin: Barnados.

World Health Organisation (WHO) (1946) *Preamble to the Constitution of the World Health Organisation* as adopted by the International Health Conference, New York, 19–22 June 1946; signed on 22 July 1946 by the representatives of 61 States (Official Records of the World Health Organisation, no. 2, p. 100) and entered into force on 7 April 1948.

— (1986) *The Ottawa Charter for Health Promotion.* First International Conference on Health Promotion, Ottawa, 21 November 1986.

— (2000) *Turning the Tide of Malnutrition: Responding to the Challenge of the 21st Century,* WHO/NHD/00.7. Geneva: WHO.

— (2008) *World Report on Child Injury Prevention.* Geneva: WHO.

— (2011) *Mental Health: A State of Wellbeing* <www.who.int/features/factfiles/mental_health/en/index.html> accessed 15 August 2012.

USEFUL WEBSITES

Barnardos – www.barnardos.ie
Brainwave: the Irish Epilepsy Association – www.epilepsy.ie
Child Accident Prevention Trust – www.capt.org.uk
Coeliac Society of Ireland – www.coeliac.ie
Department of Children and Youth Affairs – www.dcya.gov.ie
Diabetes Federation of Ireland – www.diabetes.ie
Health Promotion Unit (includes links to downloadable leaflets) – www.hpu.ie
Health Protection Surveillance Centre – www.hpsc.ie
Health Service Executive – www.hse.ie
Irish Nutrition and Dietetic Institution – www.indi.ie
National Immunisation Office – www.immunisation.ie
World Health Organisation – www.who.int

Index

Page numbers in **bold italic** indicate figures and diagrams, etc.

abdominal pain 156
accidents involving children 121, 122–6, 126–9
Adult:child ratios: full and part-time daycare **6**
Adult:child ratios: sessional services **6**
Ainsworth, Mary 165, 166
Aistear 14–15, 142–3, 164
   well-being theme
      creativity and spirituality 14
      intellectual curiosity 15
      physical 14
      psychological and social 14
Aistear: the Early Childhood Curriculum Framework 11, 14–15
allergies 36, 112
anaemia 26, 105
anoxia 30
appendicitis 43
asphyxia 124
asthma 57–9, 117
athlete's foot 85
attachment in childcare 167
attachment styles: do they matter 166
attachment theory 164–7
attachments, multiple 166
attention deficit hyperactivity disorder (ADHD) 103, 109
attention seeking 37
autism and MMR vaccination link 39–40

babies' feeding equipment, sterilising of 155–6
baby walker 128
bathing 76–9
bathtime problems 78–9, **78**

BCG vaccination 55
bedwetting 81–2
behaviour, regressive 37
behavioural changes 37
The Best Interests of the Child 3, 4
birth process, prenatal factors 29–30
births, multiple 30
blood/bodily fluid spillages 153
Bord Bia 24, 25
bottle-feeding 93–5
Bowlby, John 165, 166
Brainwave (Irish Epilepsy Association) 61
breastfeeding 37–8, 91–3
   disadvantages of 93
   long-term health benefits 92–3
breast milk, storage of 92
bronchiolitis 42
Brooks, A.M., Hanafin, S., Cahill, H., Nic Gabhainn, S. and Molcho, M. 122, 123, 125
burns and scalds 123–4
burns and scalds: risks and prevention **124**

calcium 106
car restraints for children **137**
car safety 136–7
carbohydrates 101–2
carrying an older baby 72
Casey, M. and Phelan, A. 64
Centre for Early Childhood Development and Education (CECDE) 11
chickenpox 29, 49, 173
chilblains 85
child abuse 9–10
Child Accident Prevention Trust 128

Child Care (Pre-School Services) (No. 2) Regulations 2006 4, 5–7, 120, 129, 131, 154, 157

child sickness, physical signs and symptoms that a child is sick *31*

Childcare Act 1991 4, 5

Children First 8–10

Children First: National Guidelines for the Protection and Welfare of Children (1999) 8–10, 131

children first and our duty to care 8–10

children's basic needs **70**

children's health, factors affecting 25–31

choking 124–5

chronic conditions 56–7

clinginess 37

clostridium 156

clothing, choosing for children 85–6

club foot 84

coeliac condition 112–13, 114

Coeliac Society of Ireland 113

Coleman, D. 80

colic 96

colostrum 92

conjunctivitis 47–8

constipation 43

corns 85

cot death 157–8

cough 32

cradle cap 83

cramps 156

Crohn's disease 114

croup 41–2

cuts and falls 123

cuts, management of 153–4

cystic fibrosis 26, 27, 56, 113

dehydration 108–9

dental care for 0-6-year-olds 86–8

Department of Health and Children (DoHC) 1999 8–10, 131

Department of Health and Children (DoHC) 2000 19

Department of Health and Children (DoHC) 2002 8–10, 131

Department of Health and Children (DoHC) 2004 115, 140

Department of Health and Children (DoHC) 2005 30, 91

diabetes 59–61, 113, 117

diarrhoea 34–5, 148, 156

diet
chronic conditions requiring special diets 112–15
factors that influence 110–15
maternal 28–9

digestive problems 42–6

Disability Act 2005 10

Donohoe, J. and Gaynor, F. 5, 8

drinks, suitable for children 109

drowning 126

Dunne, T., Farrell, P. and Kelly, V. 109

E. coli 148

ear infections 46–7

earache 35, 36

Early Childhood Care and Education (ECCE)
ECCE policies and procedures 158–61
ECCE settings 4–7
policy developments in 11–15
quality ECCE settings: focus on the ECCE worker 167

eczema 62, 63

Effective Provision of Pre-school Education (EPPE) project 167–70

emotional health 18–19

emotional well-being 164

environmental health 20

epilepsy 61

Erikson, Erik 80

European Scientific Committee on Food 109

exclusion periods for ECCE settings 153, *175*

exercise pyramid 118

eye infections 47–8

faeco-oral transmission 148
falls and cuts: risks and prevention *123*
farms, outings to 142
fat (lipids) 102–3
febrile convulsions 33
feeding abnormalities in babies 95–6
feeding equipment, babies, sterilising of 155–6
feeding young babies: breast or bottle? 91–5
feet care 83–4
Feingold, Ben 109
FETAC Child Health and Well-being 17
fever 156
fibre 102
finger foods 97–8
fire safety 133–5
  in the home 134–5
Fire triangle *133*
first aid
  administration of 5
  first aid kit 154
  children's first aid *154*
flat feet 84
Flood, E. 26, 27, 29, 127
fluid intake 107–9
folic acid 104
  during pregnancy 28–9
food
  factors in food choices *110*
  finger foods 97–8
  foods to avoid giving babies 98
food additives 109
Food Dudes programme 22, 24–5, 110
food and nutrition guidelines for pre-school 115
Food and Nutrition Guidelines for Pre-School Services (DoHC 2004) 115, 140
food poisoning 156
food pyramid 99–101
food refusal 98–9
food safety and hygiene 156
foot problems 84–5, *84*

formula feed
  preparation *94*
  storage 95
Freud, Sigmund 80

galactosaemia 114
gastroenteritis 35, 44, 148, 156
Gaviscon Infant formula 96
genetic factors 26–7
German measles (rubella) 29, 52
Gibb's reflective cycle 167–70, *167*
glass test (for septicaemia) 53
glue ear 46–7
Growing Up in Ireland: National Longitudinal Study of Children 57, 110, 117, 122
A Guide to Toy Safety 138
Guthrie test 113, 114

haemophilia 27
Haemophilus influenzae type B (Hib) 52
hair care 83
hand, foot and mouth disease 54
hand washing 150–3
  products 152
  techniques *150*
Happy Feet childcare 132, 141
hazard analysis and critical control point (HACCP) 156
hazards (children's safety) 121–2
head lice 64–6
head louse *64*
headache 36
health
  definition of 16–17, 19
  determinants of 17, *17*
  dimensions of *18*
    emotional health 18–19
    environmental health 20
    mental health 19
    physical health 18
    social health 19
    spiritual health 19
health education
  approaches to 22–3, *22*
  and health promotion 20–5

health promotion 23–5
Health Promotion Unit (HPU) 66
Health Service Executive (HSE) 4, 5
Health Service Executive (HSE) (2012a) 48, 50
Health Service Executive (HSE) 2012b 48
high temperature 32–3, 36
holding a baby 71–2
hospital, caring for children in 66–7
hydrocephalus 143
hydrogenated fat 103
hygiene 147
hyperglycaemia 60–1

illness
    in babies 41–2
    identifying 31–7
    see also child sickness
immunisation 37–8, 152–3
impetigo 62
infection 147–54
    chain of infection 148–9, *148*
    ear and eye 46–8
    maternal infections 29
    measures for preventing 149–54, *149*
influenza 53–4
ingestion (bacteria and viruses) 148
inhalation (germs) 148
inoculation (bacteria and viruses) 148
Irish Independent 82
Irish Medical Board 32
iron, need for 98, 105–6
iron deficiency anaemia 26, 105
iron-rich food for toddlers *106*
irritableness 47

jaundice 30

Kelly, C., Gavin, A., Molcho, M. and Nic Gabhainn, S. 118

labour, prolonged 30
lactose intolerance 96, 114–15
The Lancet 39

Layte, R. and McCoy, C. 110, 116
lice, head 64–6
lipids (fats) 102–3
Little Rascals pre-school 21
Little Tots Day Care 63
Little Treasures nursery 27
lymph nodes 36

McPartland, E. 3, 4, 5, 160
Main, M. and Solomon, J. 165
malnutrition 119
marasmus 119
Maslow's hierarchy of human needs 69–71, *69*
maternal deprivation 165
maternal diet 28–9
maternal infections 29
measles 51
medicine cabinets 154–5
meningitis 36, 52–3
meningococcal type C (MenC) 52
mental health 19
Milton 155
minerals 105–7
missing child 132
MMR vaccination 50
    and autism 39–40
monotropism 166
monounsaturated fats 103
multiple births 30
mumps 35, 50
muscular dystrophy 27
My Sister's Keeper 57

nappies/nappy changing 72–6
nappy rash 75–6
National Children's Strategy 19
National Council for Curriculum and Assessment (NCCA) 11–13
National Poisons Bureau 125
National Pre-School Nutrition Survey 2012 116
nausea 156
navel 83
needs, children's basic needs *70*

nutrition
in childhood 30
for health 101–7

obesity, childhood 116–18
Our Duty to Care (2002) 8
outing, planning an 139–41
pain 35–6
Pete the Pancreas 61
pets in the ECCE setting 142–4
Phenylketonuria (PKU) 113–14
phosphorus 107
physical activities in the ECCE setting *163*
physical development 162–4
and emotional well-being 164
physical health 18
picking up a newborn 71
Picoult, Jodi 57
pigeon toes 84
planning an outing *139*
play for sick children 67–8
poisoning 125
policies and procedures 144, 158–61
stages in developing policies and
procedures *159*
policies in an ECCE setting *161*
polyunsaturated fats 102–3
posseting 95
post-term babies 30
potassium 107
poverty 30–31
pre-maturity 29–30
pre-natal factors 26–7, *26*, 29–30
pre-school child 4
pre-school regulations 5–7
pre-school services 4–7
administration of medication and first aid
5
record keeping 6–7
safety, health and welfare 7–8
staffing requirements 5–6
prolonged labour 30
protective clothing 153
protein 103

psychological influences on food choices
111
psychological signs and symptoms (of
illness) 36–7
psychological signs of illness *36*

quality ECCE settings: focus on the ECCE
worker 167

reflux 96
regressive behaviour 37
religious beliefs and culture and food
choices 111
rest and sleep 157–8
Reye's syndrome 174
ringworm 63–4
risks (children's safety) 121–2, 123
road safety 135–6
rubella (German measles) 29, 52
runny nose 32
Rutter, Michael 166

Safe Cross Code 136
safety
at home 126–8
legal requirements 121
risks (children's safety) 121–2, 123
road safety 135–6
water safety 126
Safety, Health and Welfare at Work Act
2005 7–8, 121
safety equipment for the home *127*
salmonella 148, 156
scabies 64
scalds and burns 123–4
scarlet fever 55–6
Schaffer, Rudolph and Emerson, Peggy 166
scurvy 104
security arrangements in a pre-school
129–33, *130*
sensory influences, on food choices 110
septicaemia 53
Shaffer, D. R. 165
Shaffer, Rudolph 166

sickle cell disorder 26
sinusitis 36
Síolta 13, 15, 139, 141
Síolta: the National Quality Framework for Early Childhood Education 11
    environment standard 11–12
    health and welfare standard 12, 158
    legislation and regulation standard 13
skin care 82–3
skin disorders 62–6
Skinner, B.F. 22
sleep and rest 157–8
sleep, 'back to sleep' and 'feet to foot' *158*
social health 19
sodium 107
spina bifida 29
spiritual health 19
staphylococci 156
starch 101
sterilising babies' feeding equipment 155–6
Stoppard, M. 36
strangulation 125
sudden infant death syndrome (SIDS) 157–8
suffocation 125
sugar 102
Sunshine Pre-school
    and Aistear 15
    and Síolta 13
swollen glands 36

teeth 86–8
    caring for 88
    dental care for 0-6-year-olds 86–8
    teething 86–8
    toothache 36
temperature, high 32–3, 36
teratogens 28
    common teratogens and their effects on the child *28*
threadworms 45–6, 148
toilet training 80–1
tonsillitis 35
toothache 36

topping and tailing 79, *79*
toxoplasmosis 29, 143
toy safety 137–8
toys, no interest in 37
trans fat 103
tuberculosis (TB) 55

UN Convention on the Rights of the Child (1989) 4
undernutrition 119
University College Dublin 25
urinary tract infections (UTIs) 48

vaccination 37–40
    current schedule in Ireland (September 2008) *38*
varicella-zoster virus (VZC) 49
verrucas 85
viruses 49–56, 147–9
vitamins 103–5
vomiting 34, 156

Wakefield, Andrew 39–40
Walton, J. 116
water, functions of 107–8
water safety 126
weaning
    stages in 97
    weaning onto solids 96–7
weather, variable 144
well-being
    creativity and spirituality 14
    intellectual curiosity 15
    physical 14
    psychological and social 14
Williams, J. and Greene, S. 91
Willoughby, M. 159
wind (from feeding) 95
World Health Organisation (WHO) 2011 19
World Health Organisation (WHO) 1986 23
World Health Organisation (WHO), health, definition of 17, 19
worms 45–6